MW00564162

A LIGHT ON A HILL

[COMMEMORATIVE ESSAYS AND ANECDOTES HONORING
THE LIFE, LEGACY AND CULTURAL IMPACT OF TUPAC AMARU SHAKUR]

13TH & JOAN

A Light on a Hill. Copyright 2021 by Aiyisha T. Obafemi. All rights reserved. No part of this publication may be reproduced, distributed, or transmitted in any form or by any means, including photocopying, recording, or other electronic or mechanical methods, without the prior written permission of the publisher, except in the case of brief quotations embodied in critical reviews and certain other noncommercial uses permitted by copyright law.

For permission requests, write to the publisher, addressed "Attention: Permissions Coordinator," 205 N. Michigan Avenue, Suite #810, Chicago, IL 60601. 13th & Joan books may be purchased for educational, business or sales promotional use. For information, please email the Sales Department at sales@13thandjoan.com.

Printed in the U. S. A.

First Printing, October 2021.

Library of Congress Cataloging-in-Publication Data has been applied for.

Hardcover ISBN: 978-1-953156-49-5
Paperback ISBN: 978-1-953156-53-2

Cover Art + Design by Kevin "mr.soul" Harp @mistersoul216

A LIGHT ON A HILL

[COMMEMORATIVE ESSAYS AND ANECDOTES HONORING
THE LIFE, LEGACY AND CULTURAL IMPACT OF TUPAC AMARU SHAKUR]

AIYISHA T. OBAFEMI

TUPAC AND AIYISHA OUTSIDE OF NYC COURTHOUSE, NOVEMBER 1994

DEDICATION

Giving thanks and praises to The Most High for my life and to all of my ancestors who paved the way for my entrance. Because of you, I am. Ase, Ase, Ase'o

To my beloved cousin, Tupac Amaru Shakur (Ibae Bayen Tonu) -Thank you for loving me, trusting me, listening to me, making me laugh and still visiting me in my dreams. Your legacy lives on!

Shock G (Ibae Bayen Tonu)- You are truly 1 of 1 and you will be missed. Thank you for always holding Pac down and for making me laugh! Love...

My daughters, Jamiylah-El and Kamiylah-El (The Divas)—You two are my greatest joys in life and I'm honored that you chose me. My love for you is infinite.

My Mother, my best friend, my Shero, Iyalosha Fulani Nandi Adegbalola Sunni-Ali (Ibae Bayen Tonu)—Asante Sana for the love, lessons, knowledge and wisdom that you blessed me with. You are the wind beneath my wings and I'm so honored and blessed to be your firstborn. Nakupenda Forever Mama!!

My Baba, Ahmed T. Obafemi—You are my hero and the true definition of a Revolutionary. You are my biggest supporter and I'm so blessed to be your daughter. Nakupenda Sana Baba.

My Baba Bilal Sunni-Ali—It is an honor to call you Baba. I love you so much and am so blessed to have you in my life.

My nephew, Sur Rām Relan born on June 16, 2019 who I call RāmPac—It is truly a joy watching you grow. Keep that same energy!! I Love You!

My Shakur Family who are now part of the ancestral realm—Our beloved Aba, Saladin Shakur, Mama Mariama Shakur, Aunt Afeni Shakur, Uncles Zayd Malik Shakur, Lumumba Abdul Shakur and Wakil Shakur (Ibae Bayen Tonu). I give thanks for your leadership and sacrifices. My love for you all is eternal. Ase'

Uncle Mutulu Shakur (Doc)—Your commitment and sacrifices for the liberation of our people are unmatched. I salute you! I Love you! Asante Sana!!

Dingiswayo Shakur—I Love You Cousin!

Sekyiwa Shakur (Big Sekyiwa)—I have so much Love for you Cousin!

Sekyiwa Kai Shakur "Set"—My twousin (twin cousin), I'm so very proud of you and the work that you are doing. I will always be by your side. Let's keep pushing... I love you!

Nzingha and Malik Shakur—So proud of you both. Continue to live life on your terms. I Love You!

Assata Shakur—A luta continua! Thank you for your sacrifices Auntie... We Love You!!

Kakuya Shakur—I stand with you, Always! Love & Light Cousin.

Uncle Chokwe Lumumba (Ibae Bayen Tonu)—So thankful for your fighting revolutionary spirit! Your name and work lives on through your children, Rukia and Chokwe Antar and their offspring. I Love You!! FTL

Uncle Geronimo Ji-Jaga (Ibae Bayen Tonu)—Revolutionary to the core... Thank you for your love and leadership.

Uncle Muntu Matsimela (Ibae Bayen Tonu)—Your commitment to your family, community and people knew no limits. Love you.

My sister Sanovia Amerah Muhammad and brother, Dhoruba Sunni-Ali (Ibae Bayen Tonu)—So thankful for the blessing of being your big sister. We miss you on this side.... I will love you both forever!

My GodBrother/Comrade Yakhisizwe Sekou Tyehimba (Ibae Bayen Tonu)—I Love and miss you so much!

My Cousin Yafeu Fula (Yaki Kadafi) (Ibae Bayen Tonu)—I miss your smile and your loving spirit. I Love You!

My Cousins, Jalani Matsimela and Javana Thomas (Ibae Bayen Tonu)— You were both taken from us so young. I'm thankful for your loving, beautiful spirits.

To my lifelong friends, Craig J. Biagas Sr. & Larry Mason (Ibae Bayen Tonu)—I Love You Both Always!! Keep watching over me.

Tristen Edgerson (Ibae Bayen Tonu)—May your soul rest. He truly loved Tupac. Blessings to the Edgerson, Dabney and Neville families.

FOREWORD:
SWAY CALLOWAY

"...I feel like that man was put on this earth with a weighty purpose and wielded the culture of hip-hop like a warrior, passed through his bloodline. Old soul and heart-driven, Tupac rendered himself fearless, yet we resonated with his humanness while he navigated life, transcending death-defying moments, all of his twenty-five years."

X

B EFORE TUPAC BECAME THE PAC THE WORLD WOULD COME TO know, he already had charisma with built-in leadership skills, causing people to gravitate toward him to hear what he had to say. He exuded star quality on and off the set, and the "streets" became his theater. Always the largest personality in the room, Pac personified mass appeal still evident by a legion of followers.

All eyes were on him; he possessed an allure that attracted a vast demographic of women, men, politicians, clergy, wealthy, poor, every ethnic group across the spectrum. Even his critics could not resist listening and watching his every move. Until that point in my life, I had not met many folks as unapologetic about their beliefs as Pac.

Even in his early twenties, he was already on a mission to uplift his people. He could have easily been alongside Dick Gregory and Martin Luther King, Jr., or Malcolm X if born in that era. Much like these fallen warriors, his love for Black people did not waver.

I remember being at his home in the early '90s; he had an apartment on MacArthur Boulevard near Lake Merritt in Oakland, California. My partner, King Tech, and I worked at 106 KMEL radio station as *The World Famous Wake Up Show*. Before that, we were an emerging rap group, aka Sway and King Tech, that opened up for Pac's group, Digital Underground, so we all came up in the business together. The Bay Area artist community has always been tight. You might see Pac hanging out with Hammer, E40, Boots Riley, Too Short, Double R, Raphael Saadiq, E-A-Ski, Ray Luv, Mac Mall, Spice One, and others; Pac embraced the Bay like a tight hug.

I recall sitting in his living room with a bunch of young men for at least an hour, thinking to myself, "Okay, what are we doing here?" Soon after I received my answer; Pac started to address the room. We were all young men, and some were teenagers, others in their early twenties. However, this man was holding court and speaking from a place of wisdom that would make you believe that he had been on this planet before this lifetime.

He was spiritually endowed and started to speak about leading our communities out of dark times of pain and suffering, commanding that we rise as a people to our fullest potential of gratitude and light. He spoke on Black empowerment and how the Black dollar could advance our economic power. He felt that we needed to galvanize our efforts to recycle Black dollars in our community. Pac talked about the power of words and how they held meaning and weight, yet the overarching theme he preached is to protect and support the Black woman.

> *"The Black woman is the key to our salvation, and the world will not balance until she is served, honored, recognized, and respected."*

If you grew up in Oakland, California, in the '70s and '80s, you were probably raised with such themes in your household. Your identity profile was probably revolutionary, street smarts, book-educated, with a gift of gab. People from "The Town" had that savoir-faire, and hearing Pac talk that afternoon, I realized that he was just like us, but on 'roids.

I left his home that day with a deeper understanding of who I interpreted him to be; Pac had many layers to his identity. I witnessed multiple shadowed sides of him, flaws and contradictions like each to our own. What he helped me to realize that afternoon is that even with imperfections, you can still be a messenger; you can still speak truth to power and move your people to higher consciousness toward a better way of life.

To this day, I am impressed by the visionary he was at twenty-two years old, as his plans would eventually manifest years later.

In 1996, Tupac's former manager, community activist, and a great friend, Leila Steinberg, approached me and my colleague and buddy Alex Mejia about a covert mission to interview Tupac. Alex Mejia was the "go-to" guy; he was an advocate for Bay Area artists and the mixshow coordinator/music director of the station. At this time, Tupac had shortly been released out of prison and signed a record deal with Death Row records. A few legal issues were surrounding that company and, subsequently, we were told that Pac was given a gag order from the CEO not to speak to the press. Pac wanted to tell his story to us, and Leila urged and convinced him to be interviewed by me, despite the order from the top. It all happened so fast; we jumped on a forty-five-minute flight from the Bay to LA. Once we landed in Los Angeles, Leila took care of the transportation from the airport to the video shoot location in West Hollywood for the song "How Do U Want It." Our every movement was measured. And everything was so secretive, so at this point, I was thinking, "What have we gotten ourselves into?"

Someone finally opened the gate; we were motioned to duck down and trot military-style so that no one would notice us. Once we pulled up on a dressing room trailer, we heard Pac yelling from the back, "Yoooo, Tech, oh-hoo, Sway." Excited, we all celebrated as it had been years since we had seen each other last. He donned superstar status and moved like a BOSS. He wanted us to know that he was helping with the direction of the video, the concept behind it, plus the featured artists. But we all knew what he really wanted to talk about; he had plenty of headlines surrounding his life and career.

Pac showed Alex where to set up the tape recorder; it did not take long for him to get into it. The way he commanded your attention could be mesmerizing. I knew the moment was groundbreaking, so it was important not to interrupt his flow until the time was right.

In true Tupac fashion, that conversation was one of the most electrifying interviews I've ever sat in. He covered a full gamut of emotions. He spoke about everything from his relationship with Biggie before the fallout; how they would hang out in New York and Biggie and Lil' Cease would stay with him—they shared funds and food. Around that time, Tupac was the person that first introduced me to Biggie and vouched for him, almost like his promoter urging me to put Big on our syndicated radio show, and that's exactly what we did.

We covered many topics, and at one point in the interview, it caught me off guard when he so boldly verbally assaulted other popular artists; I will admit I was a bit puzzled, because I was a fan of theirs as well. When I look back, I realized that despite his contentious relationship with the media, I believe that Tupac had learned how to utilize the media as an asset. We see other artists who have mastered this, much like Rihanna, Nicki Minaj, Drake, Jemele Hill, and Diddy.

When Tupac spoke about his Thug Life movement, he shared how he was going to bring together our neighborhoods and help evolve the codes of the streets. That was part of the dichotomy of Tupac Shakur—Love, and War. Love for his people and War on a system that oppressed them.

One of the things that stuck with me was when he said, and I paraphrase:

"I may not be around when it happens, but I want to spark the mind of the person who will be the change. I'm going to make the hardest album for the streets; I'm going to give the people

everything they want to hear, and then I'm going to make more music and give them everything they NEED to hear. I'm trying to reach everyone, everywhere, and that's how I will elevate our people."

He LOVED the people.

Tupac Shakur passed away the day that we scheduled to air the interview, September 13, 1996. As the global community was in a state of shock, the interview transcended into a tool for healing. After Pac passed away, I began to understand why our interview needed to happen. Just like when we sat in his living room years prior, he had a vision that many could not see. At one point, I believe that Pac walked with an urgent concern about his destiny, as he was determined for the WORLD to hear his message.

Twenty-five years later, Tupac Shakur is still one of the most discussed artists of our time. The messaging in his music resonates today like he is a contemporary artist. His name invokes vibrant conversations that amp into debates about his place in music history. From generational impact to music sales, he will always be one of the greatest of all time.

In 1997 I had the honor to present the magnificent Afeni Shakur with a "Bammie," (Bay Area Music Award) alongside Leila Steinberg and her daughter, Sekyiwa Shakur. She accepted on behalf of her son, Tupac Shakur. I remember presenting her with the award, and, to my surprise, Afeni thanked me; the way she embraced and received me was like we had met before.

Looking into her eyes, at that moment, I got it—that this work must continue through me, through us, together! Much like my relationship with Aiyisha T. Obafemi, reflecting a kindred connection that invokes shared work, this book is that offering. And joining us are a collection of stories about Pac, all hand-selected by Aiyisha's circle of family and friends.

Aiyisha and I share a belief that our daily walk in faith is centered with a supreme knowledge of self, reflecting divine existence.

Ase to you, Aiyisha T. Obafemi, for upholding the Shakur legacy with honor, class, and dignity. I appreciate you, my beautiful Queen. You are a radiant jewel within our community. Thank you for the gift of your vision forward. We love you! Send your family my love.

Love and Light to the Shakur family. Honored to have held sacred cove with you, Tupac. *Rest in Power*

My gratitude to you all.

SWAY CALLOWAY @REALSWAY
CONDUIT/GRIOT

My Love to:

R.Califa Calloway~ Co-editor, Terrance, Kiyomi, Pat, Alvin
Elsie, Claude, Georgia, and the entire family
King Tech
Leila Steinberg *for your relentless works in prisons and community*
Alex Mejia
Ira Kip - *thank you for your assistance*
Rich Nice
Kelly
Tracy G
Heather B
Horse
Mike Muse
To the Bay Area and all of our artists present and past.

ACKNOWLEDGEMENTS

I'm an Author! I am so excited that I wrote my first book! I'm ready for the next one... Ase

Giving All Thanks & Praises to The Most High, My Ancestors & The Orishas for paving the way for my entrance. Also giving thanks to all of my Elders, Mentors, Teachers and Community for guiding and supporting me throughout my life.

My Mother, Iyalosha Fulani Nandi Adegbalola Sunni-Ali (Ibae Bayen Tonu)—I had you for almost 49 years on this earthly planet and I'm thankful for every day. You taught me how to navigate this world that is not always kind. I'm thankful that you raised me as a New Afrikan with knowledge of self and our people. Your courage and strength are immeasurable.

The knowledge that you shared helps me navigate accordingly. Asante Sana Mama for All that you are and taught me to be. Nakupenda Forever Queen Mother!

My Baba, Ahmed T'Chaka Zulu Obafemi—I truly am a Daddy's girl and I wouldn't change that for anything. You are the true definition of a Revolutionary and I am proud to be your eldest daughter. You are my hero and my inspiration. Nakupenda Sana!

My Baba 2, Bilal Ibn Kumibea Sunni-Ali—I was 9 years old when you married your soulmate, my Mama and you treated me like your daughter from the start. We smile when people mention how much we look alike. Your presence in my life continues to be a blessing. Nakupenda Sana!

My Bonus Mama's, Magdalen Dixon-Lewis and Sanovia Muhammad—Thank you for Always being there for me and loving on me. I love you and I'm honored to be your daughter!

My beautiful daughter, Jamiylah-El Aiyisha Obafemi-Mitchell— You are the definition of your name, beautiful and radiant. When I look at you, I see the sensitive side of myself. The deep thinker, the brilliant mind. I admire your strength and resilience. I am so proud to be your Mother. I Love You!!

My beautiful daughter, Kamiylah-El Aiyisha Obafemi-Mitchell— You are the definition of your name, complete, perfect and superb. In you, I see the no nonsense side of myself, the take charge personality. Your ability to adapt and execute is flawless. You make me proud. I Love You!

My Maternal Grandparents
Geneva Bracey Boston (Ibae Bayen Tonu)—You are the wind beneath my wings Grandma. I miss your physical presence but I feel you with me daily. I was your first grandchild and was

blessed to spend so much time with you as a child. I love how fearless you were. Your blindness was not a handicap to you, it made you stronger and I always admired your strength and beauty. You had the singing voice of an Angel... I love and miss you!

Alajo Adegbalola (Ibae Bayen Tonu)—The General, The Revolutionary, The Teacher, The peanut butter lover. Asante Sana for training me, loving me and allowing me to be by your side on so many adventures. Revolutionary to the core and I am blessed to be your eldest grandchild. I love and miss you Laj!

My Paternal Grandparents
Katherine & William Brewster Dixon (Ibae Bayen Tonu)—92 Clinton Avenue in New Rochelle, NY (pink house) was the place to be. Thank you both for always making sure that your grandchildren had a place to stay, 3 hot meals a day and all the love we could stand. I miss your physical presence but I carry you both in my heart, always. I remember spending time with you when I had the chickenpox and it was just me. That was the best 3—4 days I ever had with you both because I had you all to myself. Your love for each other was truly beautiful to witness. I Love You and I am a proud BrewKat!

Lois E. Johnson (Ibae Bayen Tonu)—Oh how I miss calling you on your born day, a day before mine and before ending our call, we both would say, talk to you tomorrow. You may have been short in stature, but you were a giant. Your loving spirit shined through to anyone in your presence. Thank you for the lessons in jam/jelly making, baking and crocheting. I Love You Grandma.

Thank you to my Aunts who housed me, fed me, loved me and encouraged me. The best surrogate mothers a girl could ask for. I Love You All!

Gloria Joyce Dixon "Amina" (Ibae Bayen Tonu), Laverne B. Johnson (Ibae Bayen Tonu), Bessie Mae Dixon (Ibae Bayen Tonu), Dr. P. Qasimah Boston, Dr. Jo Wakeela Boston Jones, Nkromah Abernethy, Veronica Monro, Dora Johnson, Nubia Lumumba (Ibae Bayen Tonu), Tamu Kanyama, Iya Kahina Ghafoor, Eleanor Anderson, Dara Abubakari (Virginia Collins) (Ibae Bayen Tonu), Queen Mother Audley Moore (Ibae Bayen Tonu), Yuri Kochiyama (Ibae Bayen Tonu), Njere Alghanee (Ibae Bayen Tonu), Lateefah Munirah Sillah (Ibae Bayen Tonu), Patricia Kelly, Patricia Jones (Ibae Bayen Tonu), Jeri Gaines, Malika Majid, Awode Balkcon.

To my Uncles who protected and counseled me. My Love for you all is never ending. William Brewster Dixon Jr. (Ibae Bayen Tonu), Rubin Salahuddin, C. Earl Dixon "Jaribu" (Ibae Bayen Tonu), Richard Dixon, (Ibae Bayen Tonu), Alvin Curtis Dixon (Ibae Bayen Tonu), John Dixon (Ibae Bayen Tonu), James Dixon "Yusef", Lloyd Johnson, Rahim Diab (Ibae Bayen Tonu), Leroy "Alajo" Davis, Mbaba Hakeem (Tio Tito Me Me), Shaheem Jabbar (Ibae Bayen Tonu), Dr. Kokayi Patterson, Sekou Odinga, Cecilio Ferguson-El, Hekima Kanyama, Akinyele Umoja, Kwame Kalimara, Mayor Chokwe Lumumba (Ibae Bayen Tonu), Kwame Ture (Ibae Bayen Tonu), Gil Scott-Heron (Ibae Bayen Tonu), Elombe Brath (Ibae Bayen Tonu), Ali Lamont, Khalid Abdul Muhammad (Ibae Bayen Tonu), Anwar Pasha "Papa Wells" (Ibae Bayen Tonu), Imari Obadele I (Ibae Bayen Tonu)

To my siblings... I am so blessed to be your sister. Nakupenda Forever!!!

Jay Dixon, Jeff Dixon, Chaka Zulu, Paul Muhammad, Abdullah Muhammad, Fatihah Amenta Sunni-Ali, Ishmael

Muhammad, Mdaiyah EfuaAta Shakura Yisrael, Kofi-Ata Shakur Sunni-Ali,

Ayana Ayo Sunni-Ali, Dr. Asantewa Fulani Sunni-Ali, Kahlil Mahdi, Warren Jackson, James Cleveland, Olosunde Ifatooke Ajala, Saad Muhammad, Orquidea Amina Mouton-Gunther, Osunsina Alaje, Ayo Nkita Mayala, Valerie Simms Dixon, Candace Sartor, Stephanie Owens, Iman Ramadan, Ishmael Turner, Deanca Dickey Muhammed and Prince Kezaredar Yisrael

To ALL of my cousins (too many to name) and my movement families—I Love You all

BrewKats, Obafemi, Dixon, Bracey, Groom, Hollis, Brickle, West, Austin, Boston, Adegbalola, Anderson, Meekins, Johnson, Shakur, Odinga, Majid, Lumumba, Kanyama, Ghafoor, Alghanee, Tyehimba, Umoja, Conner, Kalimara, Jabbar, Lesane, Cox

My amazing, beautiful and smart nieces and nephews. It is an honor to be your Auntie/Shangazi.

Amir, Taiyo, Mansa Musa, Artemus Jenkins, DJ, Natasha, Natalie, Noah, Sayquan, Lil Jeff, Nyanti, Tehura Ama, Ezenwanyi, Khalfani, Azekyah, Evedyahu, Reina, Akanni, Rosalinda, Roberto, Sabrina, AJ, Sha'Ra, Ma'at, Zumbi, Jasir (Freedom), Zindzhi (Spirit), Nandi-Iman, Surah, Amerah, Elias, Diallo, Funmilayo, Sanovia Ngozi, Santiago, Amina-Charm, Ezra, Zyion, Cadence, Jaelyn, Kayla, Kyle, Jordan W., Amari, Riley, Katia, Jordan R., Cayden, Brandon, Mason, Karma, Laxmi, Taraja, Tunde, Elijah, Preston, Lil Kahlil, and those yet to come.

My GodChildren.. You all make me so proud!
Aleah Jabri Horton, Byquan McGowan, Jamel A. Hightower, Jada Jendayi Jordan, Kenneth C. Bailey III, Azekyah Yehudah and Andre Scott

My Tribe who holds me down and lifts me up! I'm so blessed to be on this ride with these beautiful souls! Thank you for seeing me, believing in me and pushing me to be the best me possible. I am forever grateful for you all. I Love and Appreciate You more than words could ever express....

Stephanie McKee-Anderson, Robert Wendell Pinkney Sr., Tamara Adams Johnson, Odette Alexander-Watkins, Marsha Alexander, Janean Hightower, Merlina Patterson, Grace Harry, Carla Dixon, SonJa Dixon, Hazina Ngandu, Derrick & LaWan Joseph, David Hawkins, Gavin Matthews, Glenn Bozant, Kirsten Dupuy, Trella Heno, Irvette Heno Bennett, Cynthia "Pam" McCoggle, Hope Relan, Regina Califa Calloway, Gary Greene, Garry Guerrier, Malika James, Jessica Kapoor, Rachel S. Jackson, Margo Wainwright Walton, Chaka Pilgrim, Shawnae Rice, Ivory Davis, Jenya Meggs, Bonnetta Franklin, DeNea Dabney, Free Marie Wright, Tahira Wright, ObaTaiye Samuel, Jamal Coleman, Dora Whittley, Greg Rogers, Avery Mitchell, Darren "Tank" Sauls, Fred Whitaker Jr., Tiffany J. Ervin, Keshia Knight Pulliam, Dora Din Whittley and Kenneth C. Bailey Jr.

My trainer Ramon Terry (My Formula 360), Thank you for keeping my workouts interesting. I appreciate you!

My Binnom Family...
Cyril A. Binnom Jr.—Till the wheels fall off... I appreciate your presence in my life, Nkosi. Our bond is unbreakable. Nakupenda Forever!!

Kailah Binnom—You are a gem and I'm so excited for your future. I Love you!

Cyril A. Binnom III (Trey)—Your light shines so bright. I'm blessed to know you. I Love you!

So much Love for my Mamas, Norma Alexander (Mama P), Brenda McKee and Saundra Stallworth Adams (Ibae Bayen Tonu).

Nana Kimati Dinizulu (Ibae Bayen Tonu)—Medaase for guiding me spiritually and being a great friend. I miss our talks about everything and nothing.

My Mentor, Sharon Benjamin-Hodo (Ibae Bayen Tonu)—I'm so thankful that you embraced me. You always told me, to thine own self be true! I miss you so much... I hope that I'm making you proud. I treasure all of the lessons. I love you my Angel!

Patti Webster (Ibae Bayen Tonu)—Thank you for being my Big Sis/Mentor! I truly appreciate you sharing your knowledge with me. I love you my Angel!

Sonny "Abubadika" Carson, Lumumba "Professor X" Carson and Anthony "Sugar Shaft" Hardin (Ibae Bayen Tonu)—This is Protected by the Red, The Black & The Green, with a Key, Sissy........ Blackwatch, Zoom!

The contributors to this project are special because they are my family. Thank you all for trusting me and taking this journey with me. This project could not have been done without you. I Love & Appreciate You All!!

Sekyiwa Kai Shakur (Set), Sway Calloway, Devi Brown, Chantel Cohen, Chaka Zulu, Bun B, Jeff Dixon, Mike G., Rich Nice, Dr. Asantewa Fulani Sunni-Ali, Angie Martinez, Clay Evans, Big K.R.I.T., D-Nice, April Walker, Laura Govan, Jay Dixon, Stoop Lauren, Terri J. Vaughn, Ralph McDaniels, Ed Lover, Grand Puba, Omari Hardwick, Rukia Lumumba, Bro. J, Shanti Das, Stephen Hill, Portia Kirkland, Tuma Basa, Grace Harry, Bilal K. Sunni-Ali, David Banner, Whitney-Gayle Benta, Money B, YZ, Marshawn Lynch (BeastMode), Free Marie Wright, April Roomet, Tristan Mack Wilds, Kevin Powell, Kainon Jasper,

Childish Major, Sheri Riley, Watani Tyehimba, Mdaiyah Efua-Ata Yisrael, Kelly Jackson, DJ Trauma, Ray Luv, Tahira Wright

So thankful to these beings who made all of this possible...

Queen Ardre Orie—Thank you for seeing the vision and making this process seamless. You are Amazing and I Love You!

Dora Din Whittley—What can I say? Sis, you already know.. Thank you for ALL that you do! I love you!

Markeon Edwards—You are so talented and I thank you for making it so easy.

13th & Joan publishing team—Many thanks to you all for the countless hours you spent ensuring that this project would reach completion.

Donna Permell (Prime Phocus)—You always make me look good! Thanks for always making it happen. I appreciate and love you so much!

Kevin "Mr. Soul" Harp—My brother... From day 1 we have been in sync. You know exactly what I want with little to no direction. I appreciate you handling the cover art + design and all of the assets for promo for me. Thanks for being you and coming through for me. I Love You!

To the ones that answered the call, I appreciate you so much! Oronde Garrett, Jamil Hardwick, Regina Davenport, Dutchington

To the Tupac Amaru Shakur Foundation staff, board members and advisors—Thank you for all that you do each and everyday to ensure that the work is getting done!

Sekyiwa Kai Shakur (Set), Jamilah Barnes, Hilda Willis, Atisa Smith, Calandra Hartwell, Jackie Lesane, Greg Jackson, Ayize Jama-Everett, John Brothers, Dr. Asantewa Fulani Sunni-Ali, Malik Shakur, Nzinga Shakur, Taalib Shakur, Mopreme Shakur, Charles Barron, Heather Lerner

To anyone whose name was not mentioned and should have been, please charge it to my mind, not my heart. I Am My Ancestors' Wildest Dream!

All Power to The People!
Ready For Revolution!
A Luta Continua!
Free The Land, By Any Means Necessary!
Free All Political Prisoners and Prisoners of War! Free Em All!!

AIYISHA T. OBAFEMI

CONTENTS

OPEN LETTER TO TUPAC

BY AIYISHA T. OBAFEMI

This letter was written to Pac on his
40th born day, June 16, 2011

TODAY IS YOUR 40TH BIRTHDAY AND ALTHOUGH YOU HAVE BEEN GONE from this earthly realm for almost 15 years, it still seems like yesterday. I know you said that you wouldn't live to see 25, but you did and I remember calling you to say, you made it! I remember us as children, laughing and playing jokes on one another and all of us older cousins picking on you younger ones. Our childhood was unlike any of our peers, so it made our bond that much stronger because we couldn't explain our lifestyle to others without going through the 3rd degree or being made fun of. Everything we went through made us strong enough to handle this crazy life. It's so funny to me that now people are so into what The Black Panther Party represented and what it means to be a Revolutionary or in our case, a child of the movement/ struggle. I remember when our names/clothes were not so popular and we were laughed at (fast forward to you performing on Same Song video in african garb). I remember one of our court days in 1994 during your trial in NYC and we went to lunch and these Italian guys were riding in a car next to us. We wondered what they wanted and they rolled the window down and said that they supported you and we were so surprised by their statement. There's a Heaven for a G! I know that you are jamming with Uncle G, your Godfather and our Uncles, Zayd, Lumumba and Wakil. Please hug Aba for me and all the family. During my many visits to Dannemora at Clinton Correctional, I really witnessed your growth. Not that I didn't think you were mature before, it just made a difference with you going through the experience of being in that facility. I miss our talks about our hopes for the future and our many games of monopoly in front of the guards. My dear cousin/ comrade/friend, I miss you each and every day. Your words still inspire so many. I talk to my daughters about you. You are still the best to ever do it! Until we meet again, I Love You, I Miss You and I Honor You Always!! Your Big Cousin, Aiyisha Obafemi (In my Tupac voice)

3

AIYISHA T. OBAFEMI

Revolution is change. Revolution is ruffling feathers. Revolution is making people who want to feel comfortable, uncomfortable.

—Aiyisha T. Obafemi

I AM A CHILD OF THE BLACK NATIONALIST MOVEMENT AND A CHILD of musicians and singers. My parents' backgrounds are Black Panthers, Black Nationalists, Republic of New Afrika, and Black Liberation Army. My mother was a singer; she sang with Miriam Makeba and Nina Simone. I traveled the world with her quite often, from the ages of one to five. I was very young and do not remember much. My dad was also a singer. He was the leader of a couple of singing groups. He and his group won *Showtime at the Apollo*. He knew Frankie Lymon and many others from that era. My second dad is an original member of Gil Scott-Heron's Midnight Band. I have been around music and the revolution my whole life.

Music and the revolution have been my life; fast-forward to me working professionally in the music industry for thirty-one years. I started out as an executive with X Clan for Scratch Me Productions and traveled with them extensively. For the past twenty-plus years, I have been a part of Disturbing Tha Peace Records and Ebony Son Entertainment. My brothers, Chaka Zulu and Jeff Dixon, are the founders of Ebony Son Entertainment. Several years ago, I started my own company, The Blue Nile Group, and I have several clients under that umbrella. I'm also the co-founder of the A & D Agency and a founding partner of Keeping Score Media.

Revolution is change. Revolution is ruffling feathers. Revolution is making people who want to feel comfortable, uncomfortable.

It's important not to conform to society because we each have within us the spirit that leads us to do what it is that we're here to do. When you conform, you stifle that spirit. That is what society wants us to do. They want us to be afraid and feel as if we have to live like everyone else. We have to look like everyone else and try not to stick out. You do not want people to have a reason to question you. You do not want people asking why you look like you do. I've been a non-conformist all my life, having an African name and dressing in African attire. Now it has become normal; fifty years ago, it wasn't. I have never tried to fit in; I actually like standing out. My nose has been pierced since I was three years old, which is always interesting to people. Fifty-plus years later, it's cool, and everyone embraces being African and wants to know where they come from. People are traveling to visit the Motherland. To not conform means that you are willing to fulfill whatever your destiny is.

A COUSIN'S LOVE

The world is never really ready for genius. It's never really ready for the truth. The real truth. It wasn't that the world wasn't ready for Tupac's messages; they just did not know how to receive them.

—Aiyisha T. Obafemi

TUPAC SHAKUR WAS ABOUT LOYALTY AND REALNESS. HE WAS about family. Everyone being interviewed for this project is family. Family represents legacy. It is important to share the legacy and for people to know who we are and where we come from. Even as children we were taught about who we are and where we come from. Even at this time, I feel that there are more people who are more awake. Knowing that everything we are dealing with at this time, none of it surprises me. It is interesting to see how people are reacting to what is happening. Some people can handle it, or are working through it and finding their voice. Others are crumbling or confused as to how they should react or what to do next. Who to trust. Who to listen to. It is important to understand that we all have a voice. We all inherently know what is right and know what needs to be done, so we just need to do that, or relearn how. If we do that together and come together as a people, we will be much stronger.

I come from a family of revolutionaries, singers, and musicians. Music and revolution go hand in hand. My mother was a vocalist, Black Panther, citizen of the RNA, and more. One of my Babas was a vocalist and the other a musician. My parents are revolutionaries, Black Nationalists, and former political prisoners. Even when our ancestors were kidnapped from Afrika and brought here, they shared what was happening through music. They would tell how they were going to escape, through music. They would tell the time and where they would meet through music. That was the way that we always shared the messages. Music is vital to life.

The world is never really ready for genius. It's never really ready for the truth. The real truth. It wasn't that the world wasn't ready for Tupac's messages; they just did not know how to receive them. Nonetheless, what he had to say at the time was relevant because it had to be said and it was his time. Everything he talked about then is still relevant now; twenty-five years later, it shows the brilliance of his mind, who he was and his impact on the world. He had to do what he had to do then and go through what he had to go through, so that the messages could be received now.

To the artists of today, my message is to live your truth. The only thing you owe anyone is the truth. Whatever your truth is, you should live it. If you don't, you are stifling yourself and not feeding your soul. A brilliant mind, a loving spirit, an extraordinary talent, a revolutionary...I love and miss you, Pac!

I started thinking of what I could do to honor this special fiftieth birthday occasion. I feel like he spoke to me, and he is the one who put this book in my heart to write. It has been decades since the other books were written about Tupac. This is something I needed to do for my spirit to honor him.

—Aiyisha T. Obafemi

13

TUPAC WAS DEFINITELY A NON-CONFORMIST. TUPAC CAME TO buck the system, to question—which is what we were taught growing up in our family. Always question things. People will tell you things, and if it doesn't sound right or sit right, definitely ask, why? What's the meaning of this? Get an explanation. Too often, we are told certain things and we take them at face value. Even if we aren't sure it is correct or something we believe or trust. He was a person who questioned everything and people didn't like that.

Tupac Amaru Shakur was my cousin; I am just shy of four years older than him. In childhood, I was there, helping to take care of him and helping to raise him. I was being the big cousin. He always had respect for me, as I did him. When he got older and became "2Pac" to everyone else, our relationship remained the loving cousin relationship we've always had. I was still a confidante for him.

Toward the end of 2018, I was thinking about his fiftieth birthday that was coming up in a few years (2021). I started thinking of what I could do to honor this special fiftieth birthday occasion. In asking those questions, of course, I was asking him as well. I feel like he spoke to me, and he is the one who put this book in my heart to write. There have been books written about him since his transition; however, this book will be a bit different. It will be different because there are a lot of people who are being interviewed and will share how he impacted them. There will be those who knew him and those who did not. This is a good time to do this project, to have something current out. This is something I needed to do for my spirit to honor him.

If we all lived and loved in our truth, we wouldn't be in the position we are now.

A lot of them I chose because they had a personal relationship with Pac, and then I chose some because of the influence he had on them, and that mixed in with some of them being family. I just felt like those were the people who needed to be a part of the project. I just want people to know that he is still impacting the world. I want the readers to know that even though he's been gone for almost twenty-five years, that his impact is still felt, that he is still relevant; he will always be relevant. It means everything; it's just something I felt, that I had to do, that it's a way that I could honor him and make sure that the love is still felt. His honesty, because it didn't matter who it was, mother, sister, cousin, aunt, he's going to be brutally honest, and not always brutal, it wasn't always a bad thing, he just lived in his truth, whether it was right or wrong, and he would say, "I might not be right," but he'll come back and say, "You know what? I could have handled this differently, but on that day, this is how I was feeling, but you know, I could have done it differently." He loved hard. If he loved you, he loved you, and you felt it, and you knew it, so yeah, I loved his honesty, and that's not just telling the truth, but living your truth, and being unapologetic in that truth. People will be so much happier, the world would be such a happier place, if people just lived their truth. People are afraid, and I'm not sure where that comes from. It's like that fear of failing, I think, and I think that's a bad thing, because who's to say you'll fail? If we all lived and loved in our truth, we wouldn't be in the position we are now. Like that's a whole other thing; that's more than a book. That's a movie, documentary, and miniseries.

I am perfectly, imperfect.

I don't share a lot about myself. Well, let me take that back; I'm starting to share more. So what I want people to know about me is that I am perfectly, imperfect. I love with all my heart. If I'm in your corner, I got your back, front, side, all of it. I truly believe we are here to live in the light of love, so that's what I try to do every day. This is something I couldn't do twenty-five years ago, twenty years ago, fifteen years ago. I say that because when he transitioned, I was planning to do a scrapbook. To this day I have a bag that has a scrapbook in it that's not filled, and a bunch of magazines, and newspaper clippings, that I planned to make a scrapbook with, and I've never done it. Couldn't do it. So this project is all of that. It's like, okay, now this is something I can do; I'm at the point now that I'm ready to really talk. So that's what it is.

What word describes your family?

Legacy, it's important to tell the legacy and for people to know who we are and where we come from.

What do you have to say about knowing who you are in a time when so many are confused?

Even at this time, I feel there are more people who are awakened. You know I've been woke my whole life, knowing about everything we're dealing with at this time, none of it surprises me, I'll just say that, and it's interesting to see how people react to what's happening. Some people can handle it, or are working through it, and finding their voice, and others are crumbling sometimes, or they're confused as to how they should react to what to do next, who to trust, who to listen to, and it's important to understand we all have a voice. That we all inherently know what's right, and know what needs to be done, so we just need to do that, and if we do that together and come together as a people, we'll be much stronger.

Message to musicians who want to share their message but don't for fear of the mainstream reception?

It's very important to live your truth, and the only thing you owe anyone is the truth. So whatever your truth is, you should live it, because if you don't, you're stifling yourself, you're not going to fully be who you are, people aren't going to really know who you are because you're allowing someone, or a label, or a manager, or someone in your family to tell you this isn't what you should be doing.

ANGIE MARTINEZ

"Tupac influenced me on many different levels. Aside from my own personal encounters with him, just him as an artist. The passion he had, we all should aspire to that."

IAM ALWAYS WARY ABOUT DOING TUPAC INTERVIEWS BECAUSE MY interaction with him, while monumental, was also very limited. It's not something I'd ever want to exploit.

I met Tupac once or twice in a club in passing. I didn't really know him until he called me to be in his "I Ain't Mad at Cha" video. He didn't call me directly. He had someone from the label call me. They called me and told me he wanted me to be in this music video and instantly, I was like, *HELL NO!* In retrospect, it sounds ridiculous that we gave into this "war." We were so invested in it, but it was real. When Monie Love participated in the Dogg Pound video and the shooting happened, that was enough for me to say, "I don't want any parts of any of that." I wanted to stand clear and be positive. So, I passed on doing the video when they called me on behalf of Tupac. I was respectful and declined. They ended up calling me back and this time, it was Tupac himself, and I was like, *damn,* because he was this big personality causing all this drama, and I was in New York, so I didn't know what to make of this guy. I was a fan of his music, of course; I liked him as an artist, and I felt that what he had to say was interesting, but this East Coast, West Coast war developed, and it was so ugly that I didn't want to stand next to it.

When Tupac called me, I was taken aback by his charm. He wasn't charming in a sense where he was flirtatious, but he was charming in a sense where you wanted to talk to him. He spoke to me as if we were longtime friends. He was telling me how he listened to me all the time and how he knew what kind of person I was. He expressed that while he was in jail in New York, he listened to the radio all the time, and while all the other personalities were talking bad about him, I was the only one who spoke the facts, and he appreciated that. This was why he wanted me in the video. It was his way of showing me love. He also explained that the concept of the video was not going to depict the coastal war. I spoke my peace on how I really didn't feel comfortable standing around him at the time. His words to me were, "Do you really think I could be mad at the whole of New York? Do you really think that it is possible for me to be mad at the entire coast? That doesn't even make sense." He made perfect sense, but my response was, no one has heard you say that. All we ever hear is you wanting war. So, I tell him, you should come to the radio station. I believed that it would be helpful for him to come on the radio and say all these things he was saying to me while we were on the phone. I thought that if everyone heard him say this, maybe it wouldn't be so bad. I initially was standoffish, but once we talked, I felt better, so I thought the public hearing it on the radio would have the same effect.

He ended up flying me out to LA because he was shooting a movie, and this was all new for me. I had never been to LA or flown out for an interview and I was basically walking into the unknown. I went to his apartment and we did this big, long interview. He was definitely smarter than me. I was young and naïve, and the crazy thing is, we were the same age. I wasn't talking to an older man. He was just an old soul, but he was also purposeful. Everything he said and did, had a purpose. He was calculated and I was not. I went into that interview hopeful and ambitious, simply thinking that I was going to get people to hear his side of the story, but for him, it was different. I was this up-and-coming, trusted platform in New York, which was important at the time, and he felt that he could trust me. During the interview, I remember he was ready to start a war on 100. What I thought I was going to get was not what I received when I got there. However, at the same time, he was lovely to me. He checked on me periodically to make sure that I was comfortable. He was sure to explain that his assertiveness was not directed toward me. I left there irritated, obsessed, and in awe, all at the same time. I was irritated because he was manipulative. He was using my platform and he was using me to do this, but then he also discussed what he wanted to do in the communities and what he wanted to build, and he showed a lot of passion about it. He also was very kind to me. So, I left feeling very conflicted and not knowing what to do with those feelings. Despite that, I am super grateful to Tupac, because when I think about that time and the power that he had and how he saw something in me that made him want to tell that story in New York, with me. That fact that he trusted me to that extent, gave me a dope experience and I learned, in that moment, that how I use my platform was important. That moment was a career-defining moment for me.

The question of whether or not I was going to put the interview out and cause the whole city to go crazy, making the situation worse but still reap the benefits of it being huge, or did I just want to play the parts I was inspired by and fall back? Fall back and just do what I thought was the right thing to do. It was a defining moment in my career. It was the lesson of, "How do I want to use my career? How do I want to use my platform?" Anytime I think about Tupac, I think of how grateful I am that I had a chance to see him after that and explain that I didn't play the whole interview, and he was cool with it. He understood it. I was grateful for that because it was him giving me his blessing. That talk with him was so important because that was the last time I talked to him. After that, he was killed. I think about 1. What if I hadn't seen him and not gotten that blessing? 2. What if I played that whole interview and then he would have been killed? Imagine playing this explosive interview and him and Biggie died? I would have had to carry that. I am so grateful that I didn't. I don't know if that was the lesson he was trying to teach me, but that was the first huge lesson in my career that taught me, what you put out in the world, you have to be prepared to answer it. I was grateful that I made the right decision for myself in that moment, and I was grateful for the moment I had with him and that he was gracious enough to not make me feel bad about it and not feel like I did the wrong thing. He was very loving in that way. I felt that from him. In the brief experiences that we had together, I felt like he cared. I learned so much from him in that one exchange. I feel like I chose people and humanity and the right thing to do over journalism. Who cares about journalism if you are not a good person? If you are doing things to hurt people. There are some people that live by the rules of journalism and focus more on the story than they do the people. I get that, but I made a decision at that moment that *that* was not my journey in life and what I care most about. Some people believe that journalistic integrity would have been putting that whole interview out, but for me, journalistic integrity is caring about what my story would become and how it would affect the people. Once I chose that, I kept to it throughout my career.

When he got shot, I had so many emotions because of our interaction, so I decided to write him a letter. I was never a letter-writing person, but I wrote him a letter telling him that I was grateful and how I hoped he would recover, believing that he would. Everyone thought that he would be fine, but then he wasn't, and it was so shocking. Years later, someone sent me a letter, it was some museum of his letters and some website that had a bunch of his letters, and there was a letter that was written to me. When I read this letter, I knew that it was a letter from him to me. I could tell that his spirit was there. I could tell from the conversations we had in private. The letter says:

"To Angie Martinez for being true when false behavior was fashionable and for never dirtying my name on the air and for being what is so hard to find. You are a real mtherfuker from the heart. I owe you one. Collect whenever needed most. - Tupac"

I feel like that was a gift for me, because anytime I started to second-guess myself, because Tupac fans are very passionate, and sometimes people make me feel as though I was doing the wrong thing by holding on to his interview, but when I see that note, I am reassured that he believed in my spirit, my intentions, my integrity. He believed in that. So, I don't give a shit about what anybody thinks.

Tupac influenced me on many different levels. Aside from my own personal encounters with him, just him as an artist. The passion he had, we all should aspire to that. Whether you agree with what he said or you like every bit of his artistry, we should all aspire to have that type of passion. Especially if you are someone of the arts or someone creative, we long for those moments. We do projects, books, and a variety of things, and we long for those moments where we are fired up and we have this passion, and he had it all the time. Everything that he was doing, he was passionate about. That was fascinating and inspiring. That was one of my favorite things about him. He was passionate about everything. That is how you change the world. That is how you move the masses. That's how you shift culture and the way people think. You need that type of passion to do that. We crave that from the creative people we see. We crave that from our leaders, but we don't get that. We don't get passion like that. His passion alone was inspiring to me, let alone, the things he said and the work he believed in and how much he wanted to change the world. His passion was the root of it all. His belief and how he cared about the things he believed in was very inspiring to me. So, every time he talked, I would listen. I wanted to listen to what he had to say. At times, did the things he said scare me? Yes, but I still wanted to hear him, and for me, that is what a leader is. A leader is someone you listen to. We just don't have a lot of true leaders. Everyone tries to wear a leader suit and a leader hat and give themself a leader title, but true leaders that can move people and inspire people, *that* has to come from inside that passion. It is very rare to be fired up by someone. Tupac had that incredible ability to do that, which is why his loss was so devastating. Not just because he was such a great artist and he made incredible songs and he was a great actor, while those things are true, the loss was in a leader. The loss was in that rare quality he encompassed. Now, we do not even know where it is going to take us. We didn't even give him a chance to evolve as a man, *as a leader*. We didn't give him a chance to evolve into the version of the leader that he probably would have become, but the inspiration is still there. Still to this day, for generations of us. That inspiration is still there. We all long to have that kind of influence. WE all do. Unless you are a bad person, most people want to do good. That I believe. It may be my gift and my curse to believe in humanity, but I do believe that most of us want to be good. We want to do good. We get distracted, confused, and manipulated, and all these things that happen to us from the outside world, but in the center of us, we have gifts, and we want to be able to influence and lead and be important to people for good reason. Most of us do not know how to do that. Someone like Tupac, was not only able to be *that* but also teach people how to do that and inspire you to want to do that, and give you that energy/motivation to do that. Having lost that, is devastating.

Thug Life represents the underrepresented or the people who are thrown away. We, as a country, throw people away that we deem unworthy or unredeemable, for whatever reason. Thug Life was Tupac's way of lifting up this group of people that were left unrepresented, resourced, those products of their environment. Creating Thug Life was his way of empowering them in a way that eventually would be productive. So, that is what Thug Life represents to me, because even in marches for equal rights, there is still a group of young people seen as trouble and unable to be better, but Tupac advocated and explained that society made them. Society made them that way and then didn't care. They didn't have anyone to care about them. Thug Life was his way of putting his arm around all of those young people who were forced to live a certain type of lifestyle, people who were starving. That is the message, and to me, that is really important and really admirable, because he got to a point where he was hanging with Madonna and making Hollywood movies. He could have easily accepted his success and moved on without looking back, but that didn't interest him. That wasn't how he was built. Thug Life was his campaign. It was a campaign to uplift the forgotten. To empower the forgotten. It was to organize and mobilize. He was a leader who was really leading, and he wasn't leading in his mansion. He led by coming downstairs and being with the people. That is what Thug Life represented.

When I think of how his vision prepared us for this day and age, I always think of how he would be today. I long for leadership. I would have loved to see Tupac in this day and age. I think of what he would be leading us in, in today's society. What would he be passionate about today? Even if I disagreed, I would have been inspired by his passion. I don't expect that he would have all the answers, but I expect that he would care enough, and genuinely care. He would have had ideas and been passionate about it. One of his famous quotes, "I might not change the world, but I'll spark the brain that will change the world." He sparked many brains and he is still doing that. That is the greatest legacy he could possibly have, and he coined it himself. I think that quote is so true, and I keep waiting for this new generation of "leadership" to see that. I see it sometimes but not everywhere.

Nipsey was an example of this, but it was not seen until after he died. You were able to pay attention to his body of work and efforts and see that he was so truthful and so honest. We don't see that in everybody. The most truthful and the most honest, aren't on Instagram all the time. We spend so much time on Instagram, and we spend so much time framing things and marketing things and making it look pretty and important and using likes to show how many people care about what I have to say that we miss the mark. We miss out on gaining people who truly embody truthfulness and that honesty, and Tupac really represented that. Nipsey was of that cloth. I believe that Nipsey was not the only one of that Tupac cloth. We may not see them yet, but they are out there. It is the hope that this book inspires and brings out the next group. We live in an age where the public's opinion is so loud and toxic that it negatively affects the voices of leaders such as Tupac. I wonder how leaders like Tupac in today's society would have been able to speak freely and have unique ideas, yet still have that drive and that passion, without being influenced by all that mud that gets slung back at them. Tupac had a lot of counterviews, from news articles to the government, but he didn't have the power or impact of social media going against him. So, I wonder and ask, would we be able to have a Tupac now, or would we ruin him before he evolved as a leader?

ANGIE MARTINEZ
ON-AIR PERSONALITY
RADIO HALL OF FAME

APRIL ROOMET

"I am so grateful for the time we had, the conversations, and the jokes we shared mean everything to me. If our paths hadn't crossed, I don't even know if this is what I'd even be doing. I am forever indebted."

HIS EXCITEMENT AND PASSION NAVIGATING SUCH A SHADY-YET-electric industry planted the seeds, the fire, and drive in me that led to my success as a fashion stylist and costume designer."

I'm from west Philly, and if you know anything about west Philly, then you know I am a product of my environment. Growing up, I was the only white girl at my school. My dad played bass guitar in a band and also did sound for different local concerts. Hip-hop was huge in Philadelphia. Sometimes I would get to tag along and see the artists perform. This is where my love for music and live shows went to another level. I was modeling at the time and got called to go on an audition for a Will Smith and DJ Jazzy Jeff music video for the song "Summertime" and booked the job!

Being exposed to all the music history in Philly and being able to travel to New York as a teenager in the '90s and experience the club scene generated an incredible energy.

When I heard Tupac's music and message, there definitely was a familiar East Coast energy that spoke to me. I was blown away at how worldly and wise he was at such a young age. The way he held that space was so admirable. He was killing it!

I moved to Los Angeles in '95; it was actually shortly after I attended the now-infamous Source Awards show when Suge and Snoop were on stage and Snoop yelled out, "The East Coast ain't got love for Dr. Dre and Snoop Dogg?" during the time of the East Coast/West Coast rivalry. I just remember being in the audience and feeling the tension and the conviction and the passion all at the same damn time. I didn't know Snoop or any of these guys yet.

I just remember being at that award show, not knowing what my future held (being into fashion and being in that world of music) and thinking this is so intense and yet so powerful.

I was living in NYC waitressing as well as modeling, trying to figure out what was next and find my way. My boyfriend at the time was dancing for Will Smith and spent a lot of time in California, so I decided I would go out west and give LA a try. That relationship didn't work, but it was the bridge. It's 1995, I'm in LA waitressing, and I connected with a casting agent named Anissa Williams, who sent me out to audition for the "California Love" video.

My roommate at the time was Tameka Foster. She had the biggest crush on Dr. Dre, and when she heard I got casted to do the "California Love" video, she was like, oh, I'm coming!

Since I didn't know much about LA, I was like, "Perfect—let's go." The video was being shot in the middle of the desert, directed by Hype Williams. Kinda like a big deal. Tameka said that she would drive me, so we got in her little white BMW and we rode out.

There I was, twenty years old from the East Coast, in the middle of the desert with Dr. Dre, and here comes 2Pac; he was just bouncing into the scene with so much charisma. He was running his mouth telling people that being in the scene with him would make them famous. He had so much energy, and I remember watching him in action like wow, there he is, that's really Tupac. I wasn't starstruck because I was used to being around celebrities and performers. But with Tupac, it was something different; there was just something so special about him.

So in between booking commercials and music videos, I'm waitressing at this spot called Georgia. It was a restaurant in LA, and everyone who knew LA knew that was the spot. All kinds of celebrities from O.J. Simpson to Patti LaBelle would come through; athletes and music artists also frequented.

The "California Love " video is now in rotation and here comes Tupac and the Outlawz; they walk into the restaurant and ask to be seated in my section! I'm trying to play it cool and ask them waitress stuff; Tupac asks me where I'm from. I told him I was from Philly but just moved out here from New York. He was like, "Oh, okay, I'm calling you New York; what's up, New York?" I'm blushing like, is this really happening? Tupac just gave me a nickname!? Every time he would come into the restaurant, he would call me by my nickname, which was like once a week because of all the events that were happening in the area. He would stand outside in the courtyard on the stairs waiting to be seated or just chilling with his guys, and I swear there was this bright light shining on him; even when he was just doing his own thing, his presence was so magical.

I remember one time I was going to New York to do a job and I was talking to him about it and he was like, okay, bring me back a mixtape! It was so cute because it was a joke to him because now, he's on Death Row, all West Coast with it, and he's talking about, bring me back a New York mixtape.

It's funny now, in hindsight, because I am on the West Coast, and a lot of my history is with Snoop and Dre and all of these West Coast artists, but I'm such an East Coast girl!

It's wild; over quarantine, I found the piece of paper that he wrote his phone number down on. I ended up posting a picture of it on Instagram #ThingsYouFindDuringCovidCleanUp. People went crazy in the comments. It was so awesome.

I sat there holding a little piece of paper that 2Pac wrote his home, cell, and work number down on almost twenty-six years ago...Wow.

Pac and I would play phone tag, leave each other voicemails. We finally had made plans to hang out one on one, but by this time, I had started dating Tyson Beckford and Tyson was in town for work. I had really looked forward to spending time outside of work with Tupac but, ironically, I was so nervous because I knew that beyond that charm and magnetic energy, there was another side, the Gemini side! We made plans to meet up at this lounge and sure enough, Tyson showed up, so I had to dip out. Tyson later asked me if I was romantic with Tupac and I told him it wasn't like that, although I definitely thought about it.

Tupac and I saw each other a few times at different events and he always embraced me. I'm so thankful for those moments. One time I actually saw him in action at the studio. He was in the zone; nothing could take him away from how focused he was. I've honestly never witnessed that level of intensity from anyone else.

The last message he left me was him calling from Vegas saying we would link up when he got back in town...That next day I got the news about what happened. It was gut-wrenching. Processing that I wouldn't see him when he got back from Vegas was absolutely devastating. I am so grateful for the time we had; the conversations and the jokes we shared mean everything to me.

His excitement and passion navigating such a shady-yet-electric industry planted the seeds, the fire, and drive in me that led to my success as a fashion stylist and costume designer.

Over the years there are so many moments in my career that Tupac showed up for me.

The "Hail Mary" video was one of my first styling jobs after he passed.

We shot the video in the Hollywood Forever Cemetery. I'll never forget, there was a scene that showed a gravestone with his name on it. I remember my eyes filling up with tears and having to walk away and expressing that I just did not think I could handle it because it was so eerie and crazy to me.

Why was I even there; was I supposed to be there? The magical thing is, he put that together. I was there because he positioned me

36

to be there. If our paths didn't cross, I don't know if this is what I would even be doing. I am forever indebted.

Years later, Dr. Dre and Snoop hired me to dress the Tupac stand-in for his hologram that joined them for their Coachella performance. Watching the show from the audience again, tears filled my eyes.

Then, in 2017, I was hired to work with a client for a performance honoring Tupac's induction into the Rock & Roll Hall of Fame. That time I had chills and smiles. I could feel his presence.

I've had so many clients reference Tupac's fashion. Jeezy, T.I., and Nas, just to mention a few. He was so ahead of his time, so confident and stylish. The fact that people want to emulate his fashion twenty-five years later is so incredible to me. Tupac accomplished so much at such a young age; his body of work and the effect he had on so many people through fashion, music, poetry, and film is mind-blowing.

The conversations he was having back then about our government and police and the insane financial gap between the homeless and the wealthy are so relevant today. He was so connected at such a young age and calling it out! Going through this pandemic, I saw several Tupac interviews posted on social media as if he were right here witnessing and speaking on what's going on in 2021. Insane and embarrassing that we are still dealing with these issues.

I saw a clip recently of Shock G (RIP) saying that if Pac were here today, it would be "Love Life" instead of "Thug Life," because of all the love he had for humanity. Thug Life in the '90s was giving us that bad-boy type of energy. However, you could see that there was a bigger message and that there was positivity behind it. It never felt like he was a street guy who was grimy and doing reckless shit. He was from the streets, but he also gave so much to the streets. It felt

37

like it was a lifestyle, but it never felt like it wasn't love. "Love Life" is awesome because that is what he was actually giving through his message. All he was trying to give back was love.

I love you for life, Tupac Amaru Shakur.

APRIL ROOMET
FASHION STYLIST AND COSTUME DESIGNER

APRIL WALKER

"I know his vision was always about our community, and for us to see ourselves. I miss Pac. He was one of a kind."

I THINK MY FIRST INTRODUCTION TO TUPAC WAS WHEN HE WAS part of Digital Underground. It's already been thirty years so I can't say confidently, but I can remember that I was doing a BWP shoot and there were whispers of this new guy being on set. After that, we kept crossing paths. At the very beginning, I remember when he was working on his first album, and just watched his evolution. I remember watching him perform as a member of Digital Underground, and watching the progress. I was influenced by his work in a lot of ways because I think he was able to touch our hearts as humans because we could relate to the complexity within us all. You could play 2Pacalypse Now and it would still have an effect at large. From all of his music like "Dear Mama," I just related to it, and then he also had such a wide range, with hits like "I Get Around."

What people don't understand is how...in his short life, his music was able to light up this world and become timeless. And all of it seemed to happen so fast. We were all so young and it felt like it would be forever. I think that period in our lives was important because it was a time that was shaping our character, while simultaneously defining our journeys. As a Black or Blaxican woman, I think there is a false narrative that is often promoted about the relationship of men and women in our communities being combative. I am a testimony of the opposite. In my career, my tribe of men and women lifted and supported me. Tupac was part of that tribe. I was doing menswear and it was hip-hop that connected us. I think Pac's presence while visiting this earth affected us deeply and profoundly and still does now. It's funny; if you go on IG explore page and look up Tupac, he still is one of the most popular people trending. It's like he's still here. His powerful presence is not because of his music alone, but it was also because of his strong spirit. He was talking about real things, real issues, and he wasn't afraid to use his voice for the unheard. He had the heart to say what people were thinking. His words were so raw and impactful; I personally feel Pac was the Marvin Gaye of hip-hop. The passion was in the vocals, and Marvin also used his voice for our people.

I can remember one time, we were doing a photoshoot in LA, during the East/West Coast beef. We got in the car and a Biggie song came on and it was a tense moment. I was in the back and my sister turned the music up and Tupac looked at her like she was crazy, and she goes, "Come on, you know that shit is hot," and he starts laughing. I'm laughing, it was just we didn't know which way it would go, she obviously did, I didn't. And that's the thing many people didn't see about Pac, the moments where it really wasn't that serious. He was a multidimensional character. We laughed hard, and I loved to hear him laugh because when he laughed, it was like no other. And you gotta remember, we were young. I remember he and Biggie would hang out when Pac was first coming up. Easy Mo Bee used to live in the next building on the same street, and Pac would come knock on my window while he was making the album. I know what Thug Life meant to Pac and it was empowerment, and I remember our discussions on the gangs of Chicago to LA, and basically empower us, unify, and instill peace to build our own ourselves up together. It wasn't negative; it was about how we come together as a community. The acronym I know it to be is, "The Hate U Give Little Infants Fucks Everyone," but I honestly don't remember that discussion. It was a long time ago. We used to talk about this organization he wanted to build, offering the youth a chance to gain a skill set, obtain experience, coupled with guidance, to prepare them for

42

this world. I know his vision was always about our community, and for us to see ourselves. I miss Pac. He was one of a kind.

APRIL WALKER
FOUNDER OF WALKER WEAR
GODMOTHER OF URBAN FASHION

DR. ASANTEWA SUNNI-ALI

"I see Tupac as The Shining Prince of the Hip-Hop generation. He was a revolutionary with all of this fire and passion. He was unafraid to show his anger and frustration about the ways black people are treated, and the circumstances Black people find themselves in. He challenged "grown folks" and in our interpersonal exchange he was like a teddy bear. He showed love, compassion, and softness. His smile could melt your heart. I appreciated being in his presence. It was nothing short of an honor."

IT IS DIFFICULT TO PINPOINT HOW I WAS FIRST INTRODUCED TO the music of Tupac because his music has been a part of my life for so long. I don't have a moment in time that I can point to say, "Oh this is when..." I remember his very first album *2Pacalypse Now* and hearing songs like *Trapped* and *Brenda's Got a Baby*. We grew up in a Black Nationalist and Afrikan-centered movement, community, and family. So the messages of those songs were much like the songs of Bob Marley, Stevie Wonder, Curtis Mayfield and so many more, which was the soundtrack of our upbringing. Tupac's songs captured the principles our parents taught us and also captured what black people were going through. I was in awe and proud of him, knowing he came from us, from our community.

On a personal level, Tupac was inspiring and influential. Growing up the way we did, my parents were also grassroots activists, members of The Black Panther Party, political prisoners and exiles. Like Tupac's mother, Afeni Shakur, my mother, Afeni's comrade and sister in the struggle, Fulani Sunni-Ali, was pregnant with me while she was in prison as a result of her political activism. So he personally inspired me. Growing up the way we did, you can start to feel like, "what's happening here?" You have this reality you have to contend with. You have to make sense of being a part of a family that is targeted by the government and being different from your peers. As a child, he, to me, was evidence that we all would be fine because as a young adult he stood so tall and strong. Within all of the identities (including Black, New Afrikan, African-American, American) that he had to negotiate, Tupac was passionate, real, present, and confident in himself.

When Malcolm X died, Ossie Davis eulogized him and in that eulogy he said "we shall know him then for what he was and is – a prince, our own black shining prince, who didn't hesitate to die, because he loved us so." Like Malcolm, Tupac was and is our own Black shining prince, the shining prince of the hip-hop generation. A light on a hill. A seed of revolution. A true offspring of the Black Power Movement. He spoke to and on behalf of many sectors of the Black community. He told people like it was and it did not matter what people thought. He influenced the world through showing by example what it means to be an unapologetic person, what it means to be comfortable in your own skin, and what it means to live out loud. That's the example he gave. He taught people through his lyrics and songs about what it meant to be a Black man and a Black person in the world. He also taught people how it was to be of an activist family. He showed people they can also be complicated and messy but still bring it. He showed people how to be beautiful and influential. He showed the people that they too could create positive change for themselves and for others.

There's a famous quote of Tupac's that says, "I'm not saying I'm gonna change the world, but I guarantee that I will spark the brain that will change the world." Tupac had a grand spirit. When people come into existence with such a spirit, they inevitably shift the Universe. In innumerable ways, he paved the way for other artists, entertainers, executives, scholars and Black people in general. He made Black youth feel like they can take on the world. He paved the way and laid a foundation for others to come into their fullness. The lasting impact he had was showing people to be true to who they are, to be strong, and to stand up and fight against injustice and things they feel are wrong.

My favorite Tupac memory was when he did a speech at the second annual Malcolm X Grassroots Movement's banquet at Paschal's in Atlanta. The year was 1992. I was nine years old and he was twenty. I was a member of the New Afrikan Scouts organization which was a youth arm of the Malcolm X Grassroots Movement, which has a mission to organize and uplift Black communities. This banquet served as a community gathering and fundraiser for some of the programs of the organization. Before Tupac spoke the New Afrikan Scouts performed. We chanted, did marching drills, and recited our pledge and oath. We were excited that Tupac was there because he represented us. At 18 years old, he was the Chairperson of the New Afrikan Panther organization. This was the organization that the New Afrikan Scouts graduated into once we became teenagers. In many ways, he represented the trajectory that we were all on. We were super excited because he had music on the radio and we were about to see him in the flesh. He began his speech by paying homage to his mom and shared with the audience that she was in recovery. He let everyone know what she was going through and in turn what he was also going through with her. He delivered a passionate speech about how we have to continue the struggle. He was so charged. I remember the trimble in his lips and in his hands as he used them to speak. He challenged people who were "sitting around in their very nice Dashikis and having a beautiful dinner" to think about what's going on outside of the banquet hall doors. He told us that "Brenda" was right outside and that there were young black girls who were having difficult life experiences in our midst. He said "we can't forget those people even as we matriculate through college, earn degrees, get great jobs and move into middle-class neighborhoods." He said that we must not forget our grassroots commitment to our community. That stood out to me and still gives me chills to this day. This was a 20-year-old young man talking to his elders. He was fearless in telling them that they had a lot to teach youth "but as youth, we also have a lot of things we could teach you. We want to tell you what we need from you."

He told the elders in the room that they were born BC which means Before Crack. He talked about the very unique circumstances that younger generations now have to navigate as they become adults and citizens of the world. He used his own story to speak for the voiceless and to remind those in the room what their purpose and what their mission should be. Once again, I was in awe and beaming with pride. He was super cool, cursing and doing all of these things a young person technically is not supposed to do. He disrupted respectability. During the speech, there were elders telling him to stop cursing. He initially apologized but then in the same breath said "but check this out, you can't be no more offended by my cursing than what's really going on!" After the speech, we had the opportunity to meet and talk to him. I went up to him and referenced myself as the younger sister of my elder siblings who were his age. He laughed at my reference and embraced me with open arms. "You family!" he said. That became even more memorable for me because he was a revolutionary with all of this fire and passion. He was unafraid to show his anger and frustration about the ways black people are treated, and the circumstances black people find themselves in. He challenged "grown folks" and in our interpersonal exchange he was like a teddy bear. He showed love, compassion, and softness. His smile could melt your heart. I appreciated being in his presence. It was nothing short of an honor.

The Code of Thug Life exemplifies one of his major life missions, which was to positively engage young people and ultimately change the world. The code had a mission to change how young people thought of themselves and their normative behaviors. He didn't use that language in his lyrics but when you listen he's talking about how we can change. Tupac explicitly said "let's change the way we eat and the way we treat each other." While it may sound simplistic, he was encouraging us to make fundamental changes about who we are so that our lives can be different and so that we can engage the world in a different way. Through changing ourselves, we can help change everyone else. The Code of Thug Life was an actual code of conduct that Tupac created with his father, Dr. Mutulu Shakur, a revolutionary and healer who has been a political prisoner for the last several decades. Together they worked to create the Code of Thug Life for young people in the streets who may have been affiliated or involved with gangs. The Code addressed how black people in these communities should be engaging with each other, particularly as it relates to elders and children. He was very much invested in seeing communities live better, do better, engage better and ultimately change the outside world that directly impacted their lives. The Code of Thug Life was a response to what he saw as the conditions the masses of our people have had to live under not just in his generation but prior to his generation. He talked about the time and effort it would take for those conditions to change. In many ways, he was paying homage and letting people know that he speaks for them, loves them, and that he had created a plan and a vision to map our communities out of oppression.

Tupac helped people to understand the complexity of what it means to be a human being. If you ask people about Tupac, you'll hear everything across the spectrum. You will hear some people say that he was a genius or brilliant. Some say he was a thug, crazy or confused. People have various opinions about him. I pride myself on being a personal defender of Tupac and advocating for him and what he stood for. As an educator I take every opportunity to bring Tupac into the classroom and remind students that human beings are complicated and that we cannot expect anyone to be one particular way. We should embrace not only the complicated nature of other people but also of ourselves. Tupac was a revolutionary, a gangster, an intellectual, and a poet. He was the son of activists, healers and leaders who also faltered. All of this was reflected in who he was, how he presented himself to the world and in the work he created.

He used his platform to uplift, engage and speak on behalf of marginalized people. His works prepared me and so many others to carry on in the tradition and to know that we could do it in cool ways. I cannot stress enough how super cool he was. He embodied coolness and realness. He was a prince and a king. He carried all of who he was with him wherever he went and he gave others permission to do the same. When he was here, he was a very young man, and only 25 years old when he passed. When people pass on we tend to appreciate them more. Tupac is no exception. When he passed, people began to appreciate and take the time to understand more of who he was. In that appreciation, I hope that we can also learn how to look for the Tupac's in our lives and within us that we should honor, nurture and pay a little more attention to.

DR. ASANTEWA FULANI SUNNI-ALI
PROFESSOR
SCHOLAR
ARTS PRACTITIONER

BIG K.R.I.T.

"You can't compare with someone who passed so young and wrote music that you still can't write better than."

WHEN I WAS YOUNGER, MY OLDER COUSINS PLAYED TUPAC'S music. The movie *Juice* was the first introduction I had to Pac as a kid. I was amazed by the story and plot but also Pac's passion throughout the whole movie. Be it that I was from Mississippi, the inspiration and influence he had on the South was amazing. Even though the cultures were totally different, his messaging about the struggle, poverty, police brutality, and social injustice, people could understand it, get with it and get behind it. He was the voice for many when they could not speak for themselves. You wonder why we are in the streets, moving like this, and we have to protect ourselves because you put us in a position where we didn't have anything. We don't have the resources and we don't have a voice for ourselves. The people in politics don't look like us or speak like us. Pac was that voice on all spectrums, whether it was the police, the hip-hop community, the entertainment community, and/or movies.

Early on, when I wrote poetry before I started to rap or thought of putting my voice to an instrumental, I was in sixth grade, my English teacher told me Tupac wrote poems that became songs. This gave me that push and drive, because I was in the band and loved music. As street as Tupac was with the persona, if he writes poetry, that means there's another passion behind it. It's not just the beef, the battling, or the back-and-forth street talk. There's a poetic side, an artistic way to approach music other than trying to be a gangster rapper. I took to that because I wasn't a gangster rapper; I wasn't trying to be anything but myself. I was very much artistic, creative, and introverted in a certain way when it came to my interactions with people. Knowing that Pac wrote poetry and put it on beats is actually what inspired me to start writing my music and putting it on instrumentals. I was being totally honest with what I was going through and how I felt at the time. Poetry was me and what I was dealing with at the moment, and it wasn't about selling you a song.

Thug Life does have an acronym and was the first time I experienced a movement of such where it was a thing we had as a people with Pac. If you didn't understand it, it didn't matter. It helped us to understand that we don't have a lot of money, come from the streets, deal with inner-city turmoil and/or gang violence; however, I'm very educated and can escape this. This is a playbook for me to do it. Growing up knowing that many gangs and leaders looked to Pac for information or wanted him to lead them; these types of things had organized properties, and Pac knew it. We had to have structure and compassion for each other. You might be on this side of the tracks or born on this side of town; that doesn't mean we have to kill each other. There is a way for us to turn this around to a positive perspective for the inner city and community. We viewed and looked at him in that manner. If there is anyone that will make Black folks get out of the streets or figure out a way to build us up and create businesses for ourselves, Pac was creating the playbook. And everyone was listening. It didn't matter what gang affiliation you were, you listened to Pac.

I had no business being up as late as I was, working; my dad had a side gig where he buffed floors at Walmart and Food Max, etc. I worked with him from twelve a.m. to three in the morning and got up and went to school. I was about thirteen years old at that time and all I played was Pac. I had a CD player and was trying to write over him rapping to the instrumentals thinking of what I could create. I played "Blasphemy" and for two hours in this place, my dad could not find me because I was in the magazine section writing. I felt like I had written the greatest verse ever to him rapping. My dad was looking for me and lost me because I was so engaged in writing to Tupac. The lights went out and that's how he got my attention. No matter if you are painting or writing, he could get you to create something with his music.

For those who were able to see, listen, and feel the emotion, duality was a thing I learned from Pac. I like strip clubs but don't want to see my sister in there. I'm God-fearing and I need to put that in my music. Pac did a great job of trying to give you the full spectrum. Whether the media decided to show you both sides is totally different. It took me to see footage that no one else saw years and years down the road. Why wasn't that part of the story before he passed? You did not see it until he was gone. People should have definitely learned from Pac and Biggie and what that was, because in the moment, when you're in the music industry and beef is happening, it is not play-play. It was real life to them with what was going on; it wasn't just an entertainment piece, magazine cover, and something to write about. We see it now more than ever, and people didn't learn from that perspective. With mental health, people didn't ask themselves what Pac might've been dealing with in the moment of writing some of those songs. You listen to those songs and wonder, did anyone stop to ask him if he was okay and how was he feeling instead of thinking how the song would be a smash? Being able to see him that transparent allowed me to write music in a way I do. There's a lot of vulnerable moments in rapping, the prophesizing of dying; you have to get into a space not only in the studio but also in your life. You have to be serious about where you're going in your path, where this might take you, what this song might mean, what the interactions with people mean and what happens after that, and being transparent with it. Pac did a beautiful job, and it is unfortunate that people didn't listen until after the tragedy of his death. Maybe the beef affected this person more than just a diss record. That's the persona we have to carry sometimes in the entertainment industry, a superhero that's invincible.

You can't compare with someone who passed so young and wrote music that you still can't write better than. How can you? As many plaques as people are getting today, selling music was different back then; a physical person had to buy the CD. It was not like it is now. If Pac was here, you could only imagine what his streaming numbers would be. People were enamored by him because you've never seen anyone whose rap was considered gangster, poetic and vocal about social topics. He was so young, and in every interview question, he was hitting you over the head with information you didn't know about. They use the snippets of him being frustrated, talking about gang affiliations, but none of him talking about politics, his background, and the books he's read. That footage is considered rare footage. As an artist, looking at music if you're not present to explain your lyrics, then it's up for interpretation. People often create their own idea of what you're saying. They can then use that to inspire someone to do something right or wrong via your influence. The unfortunate thing is a lot of songs Pac wrote we didn't hear until after he passed. He didn't get the opportunity to explain fully what it meant or what he was trying to say. You have to think about what you wrote ten years ago and re-correct the information you sent to people. You've become financially stable, able to buy things, and helped your family, and they might have listened to you literally.

They might have done something and didn't come up and weren't successful. We have to start re-correcting the information because people are going to take it as is. Lord forbid you pass, but the music isn't a reflection of who you truly are. If you didn't write a lot of songs like Pac to explain, that will be the image you leave behind.

JUSTIN SCOTT AKA BIG K.R.I.T.
HIP HOP ARTIST/PRODUCER

BILAL SUNNI-ALI

"Pac was a leader, and he was following in Aba's footsteps very closely, because he was getting the young people to understand revolution."

M Y RELATIONSHIP WITH THE SHAKUR FAMILY GOES BACK TO MY teenage years. I was sixteen or seventeen years old when I became involved with the Sankori Nubian Cultural Workshop. It was a youth project in Harlem led by Mrs. Mariam Samad. She had twins, brother Saeed and sister Saeeda Samad. We became acquainted with them through working with their mother, who was the director of the program. Saeeda got married to a brother who became a very close friend of mine. We became brothers, and that was Lumumba Abdul Shakur. Lumumba Abdul Shakur's father was El-Hajj Saladin Shakur. When we met him, he wasn't yet a Hadji, and he was involved with the Nation of Islam. Later on, he became involved with a Muslim group led by Heshaam Jaaber in Jersey City, New Jersey. Heshaam Jaaber is the brother who stepped up and led the funeral for Malcolm X. He stepped up because no one was stepping up for the brother, and the Nation of Islam definitely stood back. With all of the foreign groups and even local Muslim groups who wanted Malcolm to join them to be their leader, none of them would come up and take charge of his body. That's who Heshaam Jaaber was, and the Jamaat that he led was the one that Hajj Saladin Shakur belonged to. El-Hajj Saladin Shakur is the patriarch of the Shakur family. Lumumba and his older brother Zayd Malik Shakur referred to their father as "Aba." We began referring to him as Aba as well because he acted as a father toward us. Those of us who were Muslim learning and trying to understand Islam. Those of us who were a part of the National Liberation Struggle, The New Afrikan Liberation Movement, and we were also the starting members of the New York Black Panthers. I started recruiting people for the Harlem and Bronx chapters, and Lumumba became the section leader for the Harlem chapter. He became a national leader within the Panther movement because of the level of respect he received. As the Panther Party developed, Harlem and New York would receive a level of respect as well. El-Hajj Saladin Shakur, or Aba, was traveling back and forth to Africa as a merchant. He had a store in South Jersey at a mall called Jerry's Corner, and the name of his store was Hājar's Hut, named after Queen Hājar, the wife of Abraham and mother of Ishmael.

Since the time of the development of Hajj Saladin Shakur, he was taking us young revolutionary Muslims as children and always talking to us about sacrifices that had to be made and that have been part of our legacy. We must be willing to make sacrifices, and we do make sacrifices throughout our life. The two most important sacrifices Hajj Saladin Shakur made himself were the sacrifices of his two sons. Zayd, who was killed on the New Jersey Turnpike on May 2nd, 1973. At the same time, there was an attempted assassination of Assata Shakur and Sundiata Acoli. Zayd's was one of the biggest funerals that I had ever seen. We had a program at that time functioning in the South Bronx called Lincoln Detox where we recruited many people to become part of the movement. We also assigned people to do security, and it was said the police came up on the roofs, because the brothers and sisters had taken the roofs of most of that section of Harlem near the funeral home. The Unity Funeral Home is on Eighth Avenue; we had 125th Street, that whole area of Harlem. The police came up there early in the morning to take the roof to be in charge of security for Harlem, and they were unable to because we already had people there. That was the funeral of El-Hajj Saladin Shakur's eldest son, Zayd Malik Shakur. Lumumba Abdul Shakur was assassinated in 1985. When Lumumba Shakur was assassinated, we found out that he had gone to a neighbor's house and the neighbor said he was knocking on the door. When he came to the door, Lumumba was slumped in the doorway, and he called the ambulance and the police. He was dead on arrival. He had been shot (as far as we could tell) with one entry and one exit wound in the base of the neck where the brain severs from the spine, somewhere in that part of the neck. Aba's sacrifice was burying both of his natural-born sons.

We were following in the footsteps of Lumumba Abdul Shakur. In New Orleans, where Lumumba was assassinated, Aba made his mark there with the street vendors as being among the first ones. In the beginning, most of the street vendors, around the mid-'70s through mid-'80s, were from Philadelphia and most were part of Aba's crew. Everyone who respected him did not refer to him as their father, but many of us did. Some of them were also following in his footsteps as merchants, as Muslims, and as revolutionaries. They became street vendors and went to New Orleans, and set up on the street as Aba did. They became part of the New Orleans Jazz and Heritage Festival and they started the Afrikan village at the New Orleans Jazz and Heritage Festival. Aba was the main merchant that a lot of people brought merchandise through to get into the business of becoming a merchant. Being an Afrikan merchant meant people were traveling to Africa to buy goods, and that is what started a great part of our economic development as a family. This was a great part of our understanding of Africa as the cornerstone of the national finance of our international finance. We learned what grows and what is being produced in Africa being the basis of that, that became part of our heritage.

In the early development of the Black Panther Party, I met Lumumba through his wife, Saeeda Samad, who had now become Saeeda Shakur. Lumumba took on another wife while I was doing time in Soledad, California. Lumumba told me he had taken on another wife by the name of Afeni Shakur. She took the name

Afeni Shakur, but not as Lumumba's wife. A lot of people say in this society and in some societies that women take on the name of the husband. That's not necessarily so in African society and in Muslim societies. Women can take the name of the husband if she feels so, or can keep her own name that she grew up with, with her family. She can also choose any name she wishes to. My understanding was, Afeni Shakur accepted the name Shakur as a child of Hajj Saladin Shakur; that was the directive that she created. She changed her name legally to Afeni Shakur. Afeni Shakur, as a lot of people are aware, is one of the most famous Shakurs. The MOST famous Shakur is Tupac Amaru Shakur, who was her son. I've been hearing over the last few years that people refer to Tupac Shakur by another name. They will say *that* name and add: "also known as Tupac Shakur." I want it to be understood that Tupac Amaru Shakur was the name his family had decided on before he was born. This is the only name that he was ever known by. The name that's on his birth certificate, or you might find it on the websites, is not his name. Tupac is the name he is known by. *That* name on the websites that is now being pushed forward is the perpetration of people trying to act like they know something when actually they know nothing. The actual matter of fact was that Lumumba, who was married to Afeni Shakur at the time, and Afeni decided on naming this child Tupac Amaru Shakur. They did this naming before Tupac was born, so the name he was born with at birth was Tupac Amaru Shakur. The only name he was ever called by, the only name he was ever known by, was Tupac Amaru Shakur. I wanted to get that straight so people can be clear on that.

Afeni had gotten divorced from Lumumba Shakur and she later married our younger brother, Mutulu Shakur, now known as Dr.

Mutulu Shakur, Doctor of Acupuncture. From that union, Sekyiwa (Set) Shakur was born. I didn't know Tupac was a rapper. One day I was sitting in the office working and I heard all of this commotion and cursing going on and I said, "What is that shit?" I yelled at my children to turn that shit off, and one of the children said, "That's Tupac, Daddy." I said, "I don't give a fuck who it is, turn that shit off!" Then I asked, "That's Tupac?!? My Tupac?!?" I played back to myself what I had just said. I had acted as if I was disgusted by his cursing on the recording, and my first response was to curse. Then, when I was told it was Tupac, I even cursed again and said I didn't give a fuck who that is. When I realized it was Tupac and I was cursing like that, I said, "Well, damn, he certainly can't say he didn't get it from me, he can't say he learned it out in the street and his family didn't talk like that, we talked like that." I don't normally talk like that, but I do. That was my first introduction to understanding that Tupac was a rapper and he was making records. He was becoming famous, as a rapper and as a leader.

There were times when we would see Tupac frequently and times we wouldn't see him for a while. I was working at the Atlanta Downtown Hilton, which was the site every year for the Jack the Rapper Convention. Jack Gibson was the name of the brother who was called Jack the Rapper and the first nationally known Black radio announcer in the United States. The convention was for people in show business, the recording industry, and the radio industry. Once the genre of music known as rap became popular, it attracted a lot of rappers, even so because his name was Jack the Rapper. It became a central spot, and once a year all of the rappers came to the Jack the Rapper Convention. One year, Tupac came to the convention. I was at work standing in the aisle and a bunch of people had busted through the door. He walked on through and bopped on by me and he looked out the corner of his eye and saw me. He was halfway down the aisle toward the stage, and I looked at him and thought, "Wow, that was Tupac." Just as I'm realizing that it was Tupac leading the crowd, I see him freeze and he turns around, sees me, and runs back, and we hug and embrace. I tell him I've been hearing about him. I tell him this is my gig, and this weekend I'm in charge of this hotel so don't fuck up, I do talk like that. I tell him not to be fucking up. It was a point where some other rappers started a fight at the hotel and Tupac and his crew squashed it. My coworkers were coming to tell me I needed to calm my nephew down, that's your sister's boy, I told them no, they needed to calm down. Y'all were scared, those guys were about to tear this place up, and y'all would still be scared if my nephew had not stepped to it and put a stop to them. You all probably would have lost your jobs by now, so don't talk to me about what I need to do about my relatives. Y'all need to get y'all hearts together and recognize that my relative saved your life and saved your jobs that night.

One of my favorite stories, when I was working at the Downtown Hilton, I was working as an audio-visual service manager. I was in charge of whatever the equipment people wanted to get during their conventions. My supervisor was actually a fan of Gil Scott-Heron, so I was living in the best of both worlds. I could go on the road, play music and travel around the world and collect the money, and as soon as I got back to Atlanta, I could get my timecard, punch in, and start working in a day or two after getting myself together from being on the road for those few weeks. One time, on the road to South Africa, when I got there, it was a brother there who had known Tupac from the time he was very small. His name was Duma Ndlovu and he was telling people how one of Tupac's relatives were to arrive on a plane later that day. A woman

68

came to me and told me how she had a young son that really loved Tupac. Her son had some type of disease and he was bleeding to death. He could survive this trouble he was going through if he had something or could touch something that belonged to Tupac. She was asking if I had anything, and the only thing I had at the time was a telephone discount card for long-distance services with Tupac's picture on it, and I had one left. I let her know that Tupac himself has not touched it; however, this is a business that the family started to keep his name going and to help people to stay in touch with one another. She took the card and took it home. I saw her two, three days later and she told me she gave the card to her son and he was fine. The issues he was having, stopped. The problem was that he couldn't stop bleeding, and when he received the telephone discount card with Tupac's picture on it, it healed him. That's my favorite Tupac story; I could go on and on...

We were and still are involved in a radio station, WRFG-Atlanta community radio. We had a program on there called *The Panther Hour* which Tupac started. People don't always give recognition to where recognition is due. WRFG is actually from our politics and from our family. Our family has been initiators of those programs. *Panther Power Hour* was a youth program, played youth music and discussed youth issues. They developed the New Afrikan Panthers as part of the New Afrikan People's Organization, as one of the most popular mass organizations for youth. Pac was a leader of that, and he was following in Aba's footsteps very closely because he got the young people to understand revolution. He was traveling back and forth, around the world, and doing business around the world. He was keeping the spirit of why we were attracted to Aba Shakur, the name, Shakur work, and Shakur legacy, and he was actively doing that. He was organizing youth, and it was way beyond just his fame in the industry by which he was known. As I got to know more about him, beyond knowing him personally, the youth had a lot of respect for him, his political development, and his political leadership. Many young people today who are maybe in their thirties and forties say they always looked up to Pac and he set an example for them. They could see him in the community, meet him in the community, and see more about him. His life was more than just going to the studio, hanging out at the studio, and going to the clubs, being drunk and wild. A lot of his life was hanging in the hood talking with brothers and sisters his age and talking with brothers and sisters who were his family involved in the National Liberation Struggle and who still are. Young people looked to him for leadership.

One of the most fascinating things I have heard about him was when some young people told me that their pastor had announced at the close of one Sunday morning service that the next week the topic of the sermon would be, "Is Tupac in heaven or hell?" The service ended in total disruption and the young people told the pastor that Tupac was on earth; he was not in heaven and he was not in hell. They believed he was on earth and this was not a time that people should be talking of him as if he had passed. We knew he had already passed, but this was a phenomenon that was growing; it was bigger than Elvis. When we were growing up, Elvis was the biggest thing, and when Elvis died, everybody was seeing Elvis. It was the same thing with Tupac; people were saying they saw Tupac, they saw Afeni, it went on for a long time. This was the first time that I had young people that I was talking with actually tell me that they told their pastor not to speak of Tupac as if he was dead. That is one of the things that we believe about a loss in the Quran. Do not speak of those who've given their life as if they're dead, because they are not dead; they are living and are receiving their sustenance from Allah, although we may not realize it.

Thug Life was a posse known in the community. People think of thugs as criminals, and Thug Life did interact with a lot of criminal elements. There was a group called the Al-Kabeer Clan, who were young Muslims involved in criminal activities. They used to call me their OG, and Billy and some other young people with Thug Life confronted them. They told them I was the OG of the Thug Life posse, and they needed to come to grips with what they were saying about me being the OG of the Al-Kabeer Clan. The clear difference between the two was, one was a group who claimed to be Muslims but also dealt in criminal activity; Thug Life was a group who didn't claim to be Muslims but turned people away from criminal activity. We developed a code of the Thug Life posse which is being worked on again; Mopreme is going to put it on record. The code of the Thug Life is a code of the street to create out of criminal posses with criminal intent and criminal background to switch over as organizations who work on behalf of the people. The acronym THUG means The Hate U Gave. The hatred that society has given us and the things that they have done to our people out of hatred of our people can now be turned around and confronted. They can be confronted not by doing negative things but positive things in the community; it is now in your face. You call us criminals and you call us thugs, and this is what we thugs are doing, we're buying clothes, we are giving the clothes away to people, we are buying food and feeding the people. I was a part of the Thug Life posse myself, and what you can look forward to from the Thug Life posse before 2021 is over is hearing the Thug Life code on a hip-hop track becoming popular, and it should become popular in the streets. Turning away from criminal activity and turning to build, building positive institutions in the community.

I love Pac; I didn't know that he was becoming a rapper, and I didn't know he was becoming a leader, but I am very proud of the type of rapper that he became, and the type of leader that he became.

BILAL K. SUNNI-ALI
SPIRIT OF THE MIDNIGHT BAND
FOUNDING MEMBER OF THE NOTORIOUS BRONX/
HARLEM CHAPTER OF THE BLACK PANTHER PARTY
CITIZEN OF THE REPUBLIC OF NEW AFRIKA

BRO J

"I just wish they would take an example of the message that Pac was trying to bring home. You can do what you need to do, but bring it home, build in the community."

T HE STRONGEST SONG THAT IMPRESSED ME WAS THE "I GET
Around" joint. That's really what sold me on his flow and
flexibility. I think he was a good expansion to what Shock G was
building, God bless them both. I thought he was a good complement.
I'm glad we were introduced to that fashion first, before Death Row.
I also knew of him through the movement, so I wasn't really looking
at the music side. For what his mom was to the movement. I was
like, damn, this kid could be something, and then when he made
a hit, I thought he was joining the ranks of what we were trying to
do. There was a performance at a school with X Clan, Grand Puba,
and Pac, and that was the first time we met and had a conversation.
It was good to hear him at the beginning and it was always good
music, but I would have loved to have seen Tupac in the same
lane as a Black Thought or Common. I think the outspoken side
of him, you know that place where he did bend the rules, and ask,
well, who writes the book on that? I want to express what I feel and
use powerful platforms to speak. I think that sparks how the new
generations think, like why you sweat Tupac so much, and then
you see them saying something very powerful on a platform where
someone's saying, "Hey, check out my album, I'm fresh." I think he
used that platform exceptionally.

I do think there's a lot of powerful points in the brother's
existence. I don't have any issue with my brother; that's my comrade.
But it's a message to people who do have a voice, say, look, man,
every whisper you put out can be inspirational to someone; you got
to be careful when you have that platform. You really have to think
before you roll off the back of your head, what can happen down
the domino trail. I think his existence is that to us. You don't need
to be provoking and poking the beast so hard that they will gun
you down and pin your own. You don't need to be put in a targeting

position. I would say, look at Tupac's higher-quality values. Look at his ancestors that were around at the beginning and you see that these people were different, doing food banks, patrolling the neighborhoods. I think people should look into that more and the origins that are closer. Thug Life means power to the people. I think it takes from every area of our life. If you are the richest person in the world to the poorest person, you have to use an edge to get where you are. I would think that he is celebrating the edge of a person. To say live your hardest, rudest, and be a thug boy that you got in you and get where you gotta go. That's what I hear when I hear that terminology. So when I hear the term Thug Life, I'm thinkin', oh, you think I'm a thug, well, "Thug Life!" That's what it is, I'll be that, but I'm going to be ten times higher, outside of the faceplate you're seeing, I'm ten times higher than that in my lifestyle, and with my people, and I don't think we're living ten times higher. We didn't have many interactions after that to keep it a thousand. I mean after that school performance we did some shows together, but when he blew up, it became a different range. X Clan was underground and commercial, so we were bouncing around so much. Once he blew up, there wasn't much interaction, and the movement stopped meeting as much as they used to. So there was no way to come home to the family reunion. Those times we did see each other, he was cool. Tupac and Professor X really clicked. They were both very outspoken. I think we need people to be more outspoken and then to put action behind it, and to understand discipline in full. It's not just running your mouth, it's like, I told you what's up, and now we're in motion to make it happen. I think he prepared the people of this era for that. The closed mouth is definitely not going to get fed, I think this generation understands that, I just wish they would take an example of the message that Pac was trying to bring home. You can do what you need to do, but bring it home, build in the community. People should take advantage of the positivity and how people use his name as a reference when it comes to hip-hop and just stand against the beast. Take it to the next level now, do not imitate.

BRO J OF X CLAN
PRODUCER
CONSCIOUS MUSIC PIONEER

BUN B

"I know you're undervalued, but
I want you to know I love you."

FIRST HEARD OF 2PAC THROUGH DIGITAL UNDERGROUND, BUT that wasn't even his song. So my first time was through *2Pacalypse Now*, and I was working at a record store, Big Time records. Me and the owner would go to the wholesalers together. If your album came out in December, you turned it in by March, they'd make samplers to get some buzz. Wholesalers would get the samplers so the buyers could listen to them to see if they worked for their audience. So that was one of the ones they gave us. We played it on the way back, and by the first song, I was like, "He's dope. I'm fucking with it." Then we kept listening, and "Brenda Got a Baby," and two grown men in the car were almost crying. Russell Washington looked at me and said, "This is the best rapper ever. I never heard anyone talk like this, tell stories like this." So the first time I ever heard Tupac, his name was associated with greatness. And it didn't take long for him to live up to it. The fact that he had the foresight, this was the same one who saw us as high school students and said we were a great group, and look at UGK now pushing thirty years. Chad (Pimp C) has been gone for thirteen years, and I remember how deeply it affected him because we were in LA when Tupac passed. I remember Chad had this big painting of Tupac, and if you asked him something serious, he would look at the picture, and one day I was like, what are you doing? He was like, "I'm asking Pac what he would do." I think it's the energy that comes from Pac; you know the "Fuck the system" came from Pac. "Fuck the police" primarily came from N.W.A., but we know Tupac carried the same sentiment. And it's still the soundtrack to the struggle. Like the song "Young Black Man," it's still a detailed, honest description of what a Black man is and how they are viewed. It hits differently when you play it now.

Thug Life is different today than back then, and a lot of us got it misconstrued. Pac understood that double standard of thug, so let me make sure I speak about it and not perpetuate how they label Black men. So "Keep Your Head Up" was a song for women, right, and spoke to them. If no one else tells you you're beautiful, I'm going to tell you, you're beautiful, you're my sister, and we're still going to the club, and whatever, but we're still Black people. I know you're undervalued, but I want you to know I love you. Tupac prepared us for today by being brutally honest; that's the one thing we take from Tupac, he refused to lie to us. He was open about the things going on in his life. The dynamic between him and his mother and how he still loved her. We just have to recognize where we are in this world, and at some point, some of us have to sacrifice something. Some of us are willing, but George Floyd didn't, and he still died. When singular voices like Tupac speak, it's hard for people not to react, and him dying in that mode, like Fred Hampton. We looked at them and said, he picked up the baton, and at some point, one of us also has to. And that's a reflection of Tupac. I remember the first time I met E.D.I. and he told me about the last Pac recording session with Pac and Scarface on the song "Smile," and Scarface gave Pac the new UGK album, and he played it, called E.D.I., told him to get in touch with them because they were talking about the same things he was. I didn't know how deep Pac's and Pimp's bond was till Pimp died. I feel bad for his loved ones, but this was a man who, if you lived 200 years, you could not compare to how he lived his life. He used to live life to the fullest. I shudder to think when he spoke to Pac what Pac said back.

BUN B
SONGWRITER, DISTINGUISHED LECTURER, ACTIVIST

CHAKA ZULU

"Tupac's music was made in such a way where it covers every emotion that a human could possibly ever have, and his lyrics are articulated in a way that we never thought would be articulated."

TUPAC'S MUSIC WAS MADE IN SUCH A WAY WHERE IT COVERS EVERY emotion that a human could possibly ever have, and his lyrics are articulated in a way that we never thought would be articulated. That speaks to his genius and his greatness. His music fits all. When I first heard him make music on his own in his own voice. Obviously knowing that he had artistic integrity when he was young, but not knowing where it would go. Having seen him tour and be on stage with Digital Underground and seeing him in the "Same Song" video, understanding our reality and who he was, translating that into music. He wore the Afrikan garb; I could see where he was going, and then when he came out with *2Pacalypse Now* and I listened to "Soldier" and "Trapped," immediately, I knew who he was, what he was, and where he was coming from. When it really set in and you got into the emotion of what he was saying or the eloquence of what he was saying, it pulled you in. For me, it was the articulation of a lot of my personal thoughts and feelings as well as my upbringing, but then being young, coming of age, and the angst and the frustration or the desire of being a young Black male, which was actually a title of one of the songs. He really expressed, lived, and breathed what it was to be a young Black man in America at that time.

When it comes to how his music affected society, I think that people did not understand that experience, and in some aspects, you don't know what you are feeling until someone expresses it in a way that you can validate what you are feeling. For example, to say you are trapped or the other lyrics on the first few songs, no one was saying that. So, to hear it, it was, I know what he is saying, but I never heard anyone hear it like this. When you got pulled into it, you just understood or could relate to what he was saying. It was the position of consciousness and street that ended up becoming his calling card.

One of my favorite stories of him, in reflection of who he was in general and who he is to me, he is my twin cousin. It's deeper than we are the same in age. A lot of it has to do with similar experiences, but being a child of the revolution, it can be lonely, especially during our time. There weren't a lot of people outside of the immediate circle that lived and understood what we were living. When we left our house, we were in general America, and their understanding and ideology was 180 degrees opposite of ours. We lived that more than we did being at conferences or meetings, so when we did get to be around our family, it took away some of that loneliness. Then you had to be stronger when you weren't around each other, because you couldn't allow the people of the outside world to push back on your existence, because it was an opposite existence. From our name down to what we wore.

As Tupac and I got older, we stayed connected in a number of different ways. In our teens, going to our twenties, the interaction wasn't constant, but it was consistent. No matter the area or place, we would always jump right in, because we wanted to be around the same things. We wanted to be around hip-hop, we wanted to run around, chase girls. We were two young boys in that space. The energy was always easy to get back to, no matter the newness of his industry exposure. His industry exposure was the most interesting. I remember him coming to Atlanta wanting to hang out, after *Juice*. His movie was bigger than his music at the time.

The 1996 VMAs in New York. I remember the energy was crazy. I had access and I was walking around with my partner, Sean Taylor, at the time, getting introduced to a lot of people. Tupac, Snoop, and Suge were coming to the backstage area, and probably an underlining part of my story and the association with Tupac is that a lot of people did not know about our relationship. They didn't know we were family. It wasn't purposely done that way, but because it was a situation of what is understood doesn't need to be explained. People who were with me knew he was my cousin. At that time, people were chasing him and eager to get photos, and I just stepped back because it wasn't about making it known that I was there. Obviously, he saw me, and after the cameras took their pictures, he made a beeline to where we were, and Snoop and Suge were behind him. We hugged each other and shook hands and he introduced me to Suge. "Suge, this is my cousin, Chaka Zulu." It threw me that he presented it that way. Not the announcement but the way he said it. So, I introduced him to the people I was with and he continued on; we went to enjoy the show.

After the show, they did an outdoor afterparty. As I was sitting there with the Atlanta people, I saw this crowd of people in bulletproof vests and behold, it was Tupac and the crew. It was a complete change of energy and star moment. Mind you, this was after everything he went through with jail and being shot, successful music, so he was at the height of his career. So, we see each other and we walk toward each other, have a quick conversation about how I was in charge of a radio station in Atlanta, and he says to me, I know exactly what you're doing; I've been keeping up, so we just started talking about something else. He was in such a celebratory moment and his energy was so high. The last thing that we spoke about was hooking up and hanging out and him telling me that he was leaving tomorrow. The next thing I knew, Nas and them were walking into the party and they shot out. He started moving and everybody just started moving with him. Street Team, Death Row East, everyone was on his heels, and he didn't even have to say anything. Where he went, they went, and the energy shifted. I stayed at the party for a little while and then I left. Unfortunately, I didn't get a chance to call him that evening, and he left the next day to Las Vegas.

I remember getting the call at two a.m. in the morning, Atlanta time, and it's eerie, because I got calls like that before. Calls of him either being in jail or getting shot. To get that call from Aiyisha, who was in New York, telling me that Pac got shot, I was like, what are you talking about, I was just with him. Obviously, him being shot before, and it being said that he wasn't dead, of course you thought he was going to survive. So, my response wasn't sorrow or doom; it was wanting to know what happened. Who was he around, stuff like that, because he was a spirit that could never be killed. The next couple of days, I actually thought about going to Vegas, but I saw all the news and all the drama, and I was never a fan of that. Our upbringing was to run away from cameras. Six days later I got the call, getting my hair cut by Cassius, preparing to go to the radio station. I got the information and I just had to compose myself because I knew I was going to have to get on the air that night and have a conversation about who he was, what happened, and what this meant. I don't think people truly understood what his passing meant, but I did. His new album had not come out yet, and it gave a whole new perspective on who he was and where he was. It was a very strange moment to have to process. From seeing him that night to him getting shot a few days later. Those moments of seeing him before something major happened. Those are the memories I have. Other memories are casual, like when he met my firstborn and us sitting in the house.

The public tends to consume the public personification of him, and it is hard when you hear other people and celebrities say, "Oh, you don't really know Tupac." That's not the Tupac I knew, because he was this Gemini of a person, and both sides were who he was. I always say, he was the living embodiment of public, spiritual battle. It wasn't that he was faking and being one way or the other; it is duality. So, if you understand the duality and ever got a chance to experience both, then you will understand. I can tell many stories of Tupac because we had all of those experiences.

CHAKA ZULU
CO-CEO OF EBONY SON ENTERTAINMENT
CO-CEO OF DISTURBING THA PEACE

CHANTEL COHEN

"Tupac taught us to be on point and to pay attention, to learn our history, know who we are, know where we came from. Don't take any shit just because you're Black. Don't think that you're less than. A lot of people get scared of other people and think that we can't say certain things, that we're not supposed to sit at certain tables. Tupac told you, no, walk into the room and take that table; you deserve it."

IWAS INTRODUCED TO TUPAC BACK WHEN I WAS IN JUNIOR HIGH school. It was in '91 with Digital Underground with the song "Same Song." From that moment on, I paid attention to Tupac with "Brenda's Got a Baby." I'm West Coast, so once he became hardcore over here, it was a whole different world.

I was influenced by Tupac's work because he was in the community. He was about politics, about making sure that Black people knew what their rights were and what was going on. In Oakland, he got in trouble with the police, sued the police department. He was talking about how important it was to know your rights and what is right or wrong. He spoke of speaking up; he was one of those people to be compared to an MLK or a Malcolm X. That is how he spoke to me when it came to certain things that were going on in our world.

In the beginning, people were not ready for him. No one is ready for a rapper to be smart and really know what's going on in politics and things in the world. He was involved with that and that put him on another level of legend. He was saying, no, I'm not just a rapper, I'm a human, this is what I know about life, this is what I'm trying to teach other people who are not learning. Or, people aren't teaching them about what their rights are and who we are as Black people and I have to tell them. I think it's amazing.

Tupac has gotten me through so many situations in life. He has gotten me through driving from San Diego to LA. I would pop in the two discs *All Eyez on Me* and it would literally get me from San Diego to LA, which is two hours and fifteen minutes, normally. I would zone out, really get deep into all his music, and before you know it, I'm in LA, or I'm back in San Diego. That was our thing; me and my girls would pop in the CD and keep it moving. I've had situations dealing with family and dealing with my mom. Listening to "Dear Mama" put me in a zone of respecting my mom. You only have one mother and you only have one dad; you gotta respect them. Get ya life together, this is what's going on, you don't have time to BS because people are BS'n against us. He is one person that has given me the confidence to be outspoken about a lot of things. I don't need to hide things; you either like it or you don't, but I'm going to speak my truth.

I was talking to someone earlier who is twelve years younger than me, and she listens to his music. His legacy still lives on today; you can play his music and his music still feels like he just recorded it. It still touches on a lot of the problems we're going through in life. You can literally play any of his songs right now and you feel like he just wrote that song last month. That is legacy; that's a legend for you right there. It's still teenagers, in the twenty-first century, listening to Tupac and thinking it is something new.

I was born and raised in San Diego. First of all, people don't even know that it's a lot of Black people in San Diego, it's plenty of Black people, I'm Black. Being born and raised in San Diego, there's Blood and Crips, there are gang members, there are drive-bys, Thug Life to me is gangster life like you're about that life. Don't step to me if you're not ready for what's about to come back your way. Don't disrespect me, I won't disrespect you, and that's Thug Life, respect my gangster.

To be on point and to pay attention, to learn your history, know who you are, know where you came from. Don't take any shit just because you're Black. Don't think that you're less than. A lot of people get scared of other people and think that we can't say certain things, that we're not supposed to sit at certain tables. Tupac told you, no, walk into the room and take that table; you deserve it. You have worked just as hard as the next person, so why shouldn't you be in that room and at that table? Sticking up for yourself, sticking up for your community, everyone.

94

Tupac's music was more about telling a story. It wasn't always rapping about money, girls, and the same thing over and over again. He told a story; when Nipsey came on the scene with rapping, he reminded me of Tupac. He was super in the community, making sure that people learned about generational wealth, people learned about buying property, and his music told a story. You could listen from one end of his CDs and put yourself in the zone of where he was, and that was Tupac. He would put you in the scene like you're in the movie with him going through every single song. I wish I had met him. I feel like we were six degrees of separation, because of the industry that I'm in. The people that I used to hang around back then, were so close, that it just hurt everyone. I remember where I was the day he passed. My best friend and I just graduated high school in '96. We ran out in the middle of the street, screaming, "what the hell!" He was one of those celebs where people kind of laugh at people, like why are you crying so hard, and you never met him? Because it's someone that touched your soul, like all the way in your soul, changed the way you thought about things in life, changed how you thought about yourself in certain situations. Tupac is everything; I will forever be Tupac down to the socks. All day, all day, Thug Life.

CHANTEL COHEN
FLIP FLOP MANAGEMENT

CHILDISH MAJOR

"The sad thing is, the world hasn't changed much from then to now."

MY EARLIEST MEMORY IS BEING AROUND MY DAD AND UNCLE and them playing "California Love" a lot, throwing up W's and screaming "Westside!!!" I had to be younger than seven, and I'm twenty-nine now. I also remember my mom had a best friend (Auntie Amy) and we used to go to her crib. Auntie Amy had gold teeth and nose rings. Tupac was on the wall, next to Malcolm and other inspiring people. As an artist and human, Pac's influence on me is understanding the range of emotions we feel and how they all make us who we are. As a person, he was a lot of different people, and I think, to the average person, we might beat ourselves up about certain parts of ourselves, like the darker sides. I feel like he showed us his various sides, like you can embrace the good and bad parts of yourself and your experiences. For the Black community, to see someone they respect make changes in their life and become more positive and share his awakening, and stand on it firmly. It influenced people to do the same.

I look at Nipsey and I see similar things, and hearing about his past and hearing about the changes he was making before he passed. It continues on now because people champion Nipsey. I think it's a gift that keeps giving. It gives you hope that when you do positive things, you may not feel like, "Oh, I can't make changes like that." The truth is yes, you can. As long as you're gradually evolving, that's what it's about, like the conversations we're having, and that I have with men my age or younger; it's about growth, and not just monetary, but in body and spirit. Having more in-depth conversations about God and who we are supposed to be as men and how we're supposed to treat ourselves, how to treat each other, and women. My Aunt Amy's love for Pac being shown through her look and wall shrine is probably my deepest memory of him. We watched all his movies. *Poetic Justice*, *Juice*, *Above the Rim*, they all are a huge part of my childhood. Thug Life, in my mind, is about figuring it out; it's like dealing with whatever hand is dealt to you, and you're doing what you need to do in the moment to get to the next. As far as today, the sad thing is, the world hasn't changed much from then to now. We have had growth, but we're still dealing with the same things. I don't think there will ever be another Pac, but we will continue to see faces in hip-hop and the world who he has inspired to be the change we need for the moment.

MARKUS "CHILDISH MAJOR" RANDLE
ARTIST

CLAY EVANS

"He showed people that grew up like him, that you got to stand on your own two and fear nothing."

IHAD MUTUAL FRIENDS ON THE WEST COAST THAT WERE FANS OF Pac, so it turned me on to his music; at that point, I hadn't met him yet. I was influenced by his work because I really felt his vibe, having that soul of that "take no shit" person, take no prisoners, with an intellectual vibe; you could feel his intelligence along with the other side. I think it resonated on both sides of the street; they were so intrigued by his posturing, and his charismatic moves that sometimes they didn't know he was telling them about what's going on in the world. I believe it bridged the gap; some of the critics might have seen him as a thug, but when their kids started listening and learning the music, it snuck in the house. Back to that spirit of a rider, with what's going on in the world, it connects to being oppressed, and having that spirit of turning nothing into something. He made the best out of everything around him. As a man who lived that life, it impressed upon me to keep striving, and to be outspoken, but at the same time, speak with intelligent thought. It gave you another way to kick the door down. If you listen to his music, you can see he's a well-read man, so you had to press upon the intellectual side above everything. He showed people that grew up like him that you got to stand on your own two and fear nothing.

First time I heard Tupac, I think I was in the AUC. I came from a dancer background so I was checking him out with Digital Underground, and his verses stood out. I could see that energy he came with. So I was wondering who that is; he was hard. At that time, I didn't know who Tupac was, but I knew I liked his verse on "Same Song". To see him on stage performing that verse, was the epitome of Black Power. Pac came to Atlanta, we had been kickin' it all week, it's so funny. I was introduced to Pac by Dedan and Stretch. One time I was at a show with Goodie Mob, and Pac was getting ready to perform, and we heard "Hootie Hoo." I was familiar with Goodie Mob but not really. I knew a few people, but you hear "Hootie Hoo," and you see about twenty to thirty deep come into the club, and Pac said, "They the truth," that's Goodie Mob, Outkast. Pac goes, "Yeah, they're hard." They come in and, mind you, you can see their energy, and the rage could be seen on that stage. Someone had thrown water on Pac, and he stepped to him. We gave him a greeting; Pac was the first one off the stage, so I knew then he for real. When we followed him off the stage, I introduced him to one of my partners, Play, who is now deceased. Rest both of their souls.

We went to Nikki's, a strip club on Stewart Avenue. Actually, it's a show store in Atlanta, where the girls show their shoes off. An associate got into it with one of the young ladies, and they went back and forth, and the young lady called the police and said Tupac hit her, because she knew the urgency if she said Pac did it, and he was nowhere near the situation. So, we were held up in the club, and the reporters came, and the news was spreading that Tupac got into an altercation in the nightclub, which was false. It would have never been him in that situation. I looked at it like, wow, the media can create another narrative about you, and how easily people buy into it because when you get to a certain level, you become a target. He was moving like a regular dude, but that was the turning point where he wasn't going to be regular anymore. People realized he was a star.

What goes up, must come down; that's the theory of relativity. I've never feared anyone going higher than me. One of my interns became my boss. So, I'm a firm believer in how you treat people, how you manifest, and that comes back to Pac. I saw how he treated a bum, the same way he treated a superstar. In your mind, if you don't move like that, it's going to be a lonely road up top, and once you're up top, you're going to be so damn lonely, because you cut everybody off and you didn't make room for someone else to climb.

Everybody is always looking for help, and someone is saying, "What am I going to get out of it?" I've never had that thought of monetary value or...We all like flowers, and I like to give my flowers while people are living, and I like to receive my flowers while I'm living. You don't want your funeral to come around and nobody shows up. In life, death is guaranteed, so how you set your table before you leave dictates a lot about you. You have to help somebody else. I tell cats I never got into this to make the most money in the world. I'm happy within my soul, my spirit, and that allows me not to compromise myself. Finances make a lot of people compromise themselves. There are people who sell their soul for material things.

Thug Life to me is you being who you are, and not taking any shit, and I don't mean that in a violent way. I mean that in knowing your self-worth and not changing according to how society may dictate. A lot of people always want to take that "I'm the boss" role, and Thug Life represents playing your position to become the boss. You have to be a good, loyal soldier; real soldier. You have to guard yourself; you have to build yourself up mentally, strengthen your mind and body. Those real Thug Life thoughts to me, it's me seeing the oppressed rising up and having no regrets of why they are speaking out, because if you have been oppressed, do you stay oppressed or do you survive? You know, I'm a bona fide survivor, so...it's kind of hard to explain it because I'm a man that lives it; I came from nothing to something, and I think that's the mission, come from nothing and create something for yourself. It's that warrior mentality.

CLAY EVANS
MANAGER/RUBICON

DAVID BANNER

"When people compare Tupac to other artists, I think that's flawed. He was bigger than rap. He influenced people all over the world who may not even like rap music."

IDON'T REMEMBER EXACTLY WHEN I WAS INTRODUCED TO TUPAC, but what I do know is that it started early and his music had a great effect on me. The funny thing about it is, the initial Pac that everybody liked? I sorta missed those years. I was a *2Pacalypse Now* fan, before Death Row. "Soulja's Story," that's the Pac that I fell in love with. I was so enthralled with hip-hop in general at the time when Pac came out. But his storytelling and his passion were game-changing for me. He would say stuff that other people wouldn't say, and would say it with a level of conviction that you barely saw in people our parents' age. I got into an argument with a young lady during the pandemic who made a joke about "Brenda's Got a Baby." When they first started giving out the stimulus checks, she posted a meme that said, "I bet you Brenda wish she woulda kept that kid for $1400." And I said, "That shit ain't funny! Do you even know the song? She put the baby in the trash! That shit ain't funny!" That detail in the story showed me the dexterity and the depth Tupac possessed. He didn't just say she put the baby up for adoption. The vividness of the story, as soon as I heard that, I was like, "That ain't nothing to play with."

It's funny, I hate to admit this, but I really came back around as a fan right around *Makaveli*.

Pac was one of the biggest influences in my life, not just musically. I've never been influenced by other people. I'm not one of these guys who follows the crowd; I usually run away from the crowd. So, Pac is the only person, the only artist that made me do something just because I saw them do it. I started smoking cigarettes because of Tupac. And I hate cigarettes and cigarette smoke. He just looked so cool with the Newport in his mouth. It was funny; I was a chain smoker: once I would smoke one, I would smoke five. Then I could go for two, three days without smoking. One day I asked my assistant, Graham, to get me a pack of cigarettes. He grabbed my arm and pointed to the tattoo I got for my father and said, "I don't wanna put you on MY arm." My father died of lung and brain cancer. The moment Graham told me that, I cut the cigarettes.

What influenced me about his work was more the revolutionary side. That's the biggest gripe that I have about Pac's legacy. Everybody wants the style, the bravado, the stuff that's cool in the streets. But you can't talk about Pac without talking about revolution, without connecting the people, without discussing his code of ethics. Pac and Goodie Mob were the ones who showed me it's all right to be both. I do have history; I do get down in very aggressive ways at times. That doesn't make me any less godly; that doesn't make me any less passionate about my people. It doesn't make me any less revolutionary. When I started changing my life and the things that I talked about, the things that I stood for, I noticed that a lot of my peers were uncomfortable. But you gotta think: if people who act like me are the hottest artists out there, that means everybody else has to start acting like. At the height of my career, I remember going to a city I used to go to a lot and saying, "Y'all are making it rain in the club; why the fuck can't you make it rain in the hood?" So I started going around and giving back to that community. The rappers from that city had to follow suit because, "The hottest dude from Mississippi can't come to our town doing more than we do." So I peer-pressured them into action, and that's fine: I don't care WHY it happens. A lot of times, we evolve, and even our own people don't feel comfortable. Because if that's the man that we have to compare ourselves to, then that puts a lot of pressure on us. I think that's what made people uncomfortable about the revolutionary aspects of who Pac was.

One of the things I fear as a vocal Black man in America is that Black people in America are waiting for Jesus to come. And I don't think no white man is gonna come out of the sky. If Jesus does exist in the capacity that we think Jesus existed, then why would he come help us when he gave us everything that you need? You can do it for yourself. When people try to elevate artists to this Jesus-like figure—like *Makaveli*—they just sit back and watch that artist on the cross, so to speak. The same way people said, "Jesus was my savior." Then why the hell did you let him stay up on that cross? You could've taken him down! It was more of y'all than them! I see the same thing with artists: they watch artists be depressed, and then when they die, it's, "Aww, we miss him." No, you could have done something when they were here and you didn't. You sat back and watched that fuck shit happen and did nothing about it.

I just think if we really are talking about the spirit of Tupac, we shouldn't let the same thing happen to those people who remind you of that spirit. If we really love Pac like we say we do, when you recognize that spirit in the next generation, or you see a young person make some of the mistakes Pac may have made, then we need to stop that as soon as we see it.

When people compare Tupac to other artists and try to leverage how big he was in rap, I think that's flawed. I think he was bigger than rap. He influenced people all over the world who may not even like rap music. I'm honored to be able to be a part of his family's legacy. It lets me know where I'm at in my life for you all to even deem me worthy to be a part of this conversation, knowing how much he meant to me, is an honor.

LAVELL (DAVID BANNER) CRUMP
CEO OF A BANNER VISION
BUSINESSMAN
ACTIVIST

DEVI BROWN

"With Deepak, I've learned to meditate, the gifts of self-awareness, how to observe myself and come into peace. From Pac, I embraced the freedom to be curious about myself and investigative about the world around me and the beliefs I held."

IFEEL LIKE THERE IS SO MUCH TO SAY AND YET, THE FIRST THING I know I want to say is that I am so grateful for the life of Tupac Shakur. That is what I want to center this conversation around. I grew up as a fan of Tupac. He died when I was young, but the resounding effect that Tupac had on me still echoes throughout my life, and his being really was the catalyst for me living life as that of a "seeker." I remember hearing his music and the way I connected to it, it was as if he was leaving a trail to help me learn about the world. To aid me in finding out more about myself. Each one of his songs felt so intentionally crafted. It was a jam, sounded great on the radio, AND it was filled with these bread crumbs in the things that he said, leading you inward. A trail that took you to a new level of yourself.

I was a young girl when I first learned about Tupac. I was about nine or ten years old. Growing up in LA at that time, Tupac was king. He was super saturated on the radio and I remember hearing his song "So Many Tears." I heard this song and it felt like he was giving this access to understanding human emotion, more fully and more deeply. Even at that age, I fully resonated with that song. I resonated with that message of having all of these seeds of nourishment and emotions and asking myself, "What are these feelings? What is this perspective? I want to know more about it." "So Many Tears" was that gateway to the Tupac insight. Other songs that introduced me to him were also "Dear Mama" and "California Love." "To Live and Die in LA" was definitely one of them, being from LA. One of my lifelong favorites was "Picture Me Rollin'." This was one of the first songs I learned by heart. I remember feeling so proud about that. I saved all my allowance money once and I got one of his double-disk albums. We were on a family trip going somewhere, and I remember being in the back seat for hours with my Walkman, in my own world, feeling as though I was in conversation with Pac. Listening to it made me feel as though he was teaching me these big lessons as I listened to the music over and over again.

I did a school project when I was thirteen years old on Pac, and it got featured in our school library for years. It was a project around his poetry and how I was connecting to the deeper meanings of everything that he said. I felt so inspired to be more. To me, Pac's music, poetry, and way of being connected to me because he seemed so self-sovereign. He really knew who he was, but not in any egoic way, which is contrary to what we see in hip-hop. Not to say that he was without ego, but there was this emphasis put on things in music at the time. There was this big emphasis on luxury goods, drugs, women, and what you were wearing. Pac, on the other hand, kept his music more nourishing, even when he did discuss those things. His music always had something in it for you that would supersede any trend in time. There were real life lessons and real clear perspectives. When I was first connecting to his music, that's what I connected to. It was this sacred permission to be multifaceted.

One of Pac's interviews from *MTV News* gets played a lot. In this video he says, "I may not change the world, but I guarantee I will spark the brain that does." I remember hearing that quote in real time, and completely agreeing with his entire statement. Even now, looking back, twenty-five years later, and realizing that, *that* is exactly what he was doing and what he did. I feel like my brain is sparked and my desire to show up for other people, to speak my truth, to have a life of being informed and having access to all kinds of different things. Tupac was my spark for that. If that happened for me, we clearly see that spark in Kendrick and so many of the leading powerful voices in the world. Tupac prophesied over his own life and it became real.

Tupac made so many contributions to the world. Nothing existed like Pac before Pac and nothing will exist after. However, you see the clear influence he had on what came after him. Pac was the first Black man I saw who encompassed so many things at once. When we reflect, we see that he was so many things, but it also meant that sometimes, there were still these conflicting ideals happening at once. There were certain conversations of women in the music that felt misogynistic, but at the same time, he had some of the most uplifting songs that ever existed for women. I love those polarities. I feel that he really represents the two polarities of divine masculine and divine feminine. He was very supportive, loving and nurturing with women. The way he empathized with the plight of women at such a young age was unreal. That's what blows me away. In my mind, Pac wasn't human. There was something very godly different and special about him, like he had this anointing. When I think of how I viewed him in these multiple polarities and in these specific kinds of themes, and put that all in the framework of he was under twenty-four. He was under twenty-four, creating and making all of these things. It bears the question of, "How did you have access to that much of yourself that young?" You saw that he had access to so many parts of him and at the same time, he was so young. All these facets of who he was are typically revealed to people over time.

When we sit and really experience the gravity of what his life meant. Peeling back those small layers of "How were you all these things so young?" There are pieces of his wisdom that people usually access at the age of fifty, or when you have lived this kind of life experience. He had access to so much of him, way more than anyone has or have, and there are wonderful and phenomenal people that are changing the world every day, but not in the recipe of him. Not in the way that he was. He knew there was this urgency

117

on his calling and he was showing up for it and meeting it. Tupac being his age and knowing and having peace with understanding his time on earth would be short-lived but yet impactful is mind-blowing. When we think of the limited box of hip-hop and legacy, we think of just music, but Tupac was so many things. Hip-hop and music was one expression of his destiny. I personally don't even care to let someone talk Pac with me, because unless you understand the fullness of this life, I am not going to debate something as small as "Biggie or Tupac" because it is pointless and silly, because they are so different and not comparable. In order for me to have any kind of discussion like that, I have to know that you understand God and that you understand divine calling and what a paradigm-shifting way of being really is.

When we think of Pac's catalog, all of it gives insight to his deeper thoughts and his psyche and understanding on how he sees the world. Even the songs that were about sex and Hennessy. That always came through. I remembered when one of my best friends was murdered, and I remember listening to "Baby Don't Cry" on repeat. There were songs that connected to me so strongly, and at that age, going through that experience and not having the tools then, his album gave me language. It gave me a deeper understanding of what I was feeling and how to express it. As well as why we saw dynamics that we saw in the areas that we grew up. He was this sage, this guide. At this age I better understand why I feel so fierce about his legacy. His life was sacred. His work is so much more than being a simple legacy or body of work. It was a sacred practice and revelations that were coming from him. I feel like Pac's work was in service to the elevation to our collective consciousness, and you cannot say that about everyone.

For me, when I think of the term Thug Life and I think of the way he used to say it and how I heard it, it felt like an essence of self-sovereignty. It really felt like someone who was so clear on who they were and able to make all choices out of the seed of that knowing. Thug Life to me is waving that flag of "I know exactly who I am and I am going to continue to show up that way with my values, with my ideals that I know were God-given and gifted to me to be expressed." This interview has given me deeper insight as to why I felt so strongly about him.

When we think of this exact moment in time and some of the things that are really good for so many of us is the very clear calling out of the iniquity that exists in the world. Right now, for the first time in human history, as a grand collective, we are calling out the silencing of women. We are calling out all the structures of oppression, societally, systemically, within our socioeconomic status and makeup, and it is so fucking freeing to feel and incredible for us. There is this freedom, and we are publicly expressing and calling out some of the most limiting behaviors and limiting systems that have existed in humanity. When we look at his body of work, everything that we are collectively echoing right now, he was saying it in all of his songs, but we were not caught up in his songs. We could hear what he was saying, but we weren't really able to understand and live the reversals of those noticings. We weren't in a space where as a group of thousands, millions, were seeing it at the same time and demanding change and demanding growth and acknowledgment. In all of his songs, he was doing that. Even when thinking of how he made songs titled "Brenda Got a Baby," "Keep Your Head Up," "Baby Don't Cry," everything said in those songs is in service to the women's movement we've seen expanding in the last five years. Speaking directly on a song as a rapper, with a record being played on the radio about rape, men treating women in ways that are devastating and are unequal. He spoke about child pregnancy, but what are some of the factors that a woman at a young age can find herself pregnant? What are some of the holding accountable of the men? He was calling it all out on songs in ways that no one else ever has, but absolutely no one else was at that time. The gifts of his life are just so many.

If we really get into the fibers of what his legacy meant, it is so much deeper than how many albums and the prolific body of work he left behind, the artistry and the plans he left behind to build. It's bigger than the movie career; it's bigger than the books. He planted seeds twenty years ago that are actively being harvested, understood, and explored right now. Who else's music has done that? What rap musician has done that? I am not saying that as a calling out or trying to be too comparative, but I am simply saying that is the greatness of his life. Even saying it now, out loud, gives me chills. I feel so grateful. There is a song by Don Kennedy and he starts the song with, "I am grateful for the life of Tupac Shakur;" that is the way he goes into this song and that is truly how I feel, so much of the time. I feel grateful to feel *that* and not have known him and not really gifted with the opportunity to have met him but yet still feel that depth of impact and inspiration. All of God's whispers and the way that God leads you to you but leads you to deepening however you are meant to be in the world, and one day I was sharing with a friend how it is so crazy, when we sink into the noticing of what makes us us. In 2014, I just started sharing my meditation practice with my radio audience, and this newspaper where I was living did a feature on me. When they came to my house, it was 100 percent Pac. You just saw Pac everywhere. When the article came out, the title was, "Tupac Meets Deepak with LA Style."

I remember when that article came out, I was so excited because I thought the title fit me perfectly. Just the other day, I was looking at the article in the frame, with new eyes in such reverence, like God was letting me know where I was headed and what my greatest influences were. When I think about my life, I don't know where I would be without the influence of Tupac and Deepak. I have no idea who I would be. With Deepak, I've learned to meditate, the gifts of self-awareness, how to observe myself and come into peace. From Pac, I embraced the freedom to be curious about myself and investigative about the world around me and the beliefs I held. In every song he was an explorer of himself and humanity. In all of his songs, he was connected to investigating who he was and to living in self inquiry. He expressed that, and it is so interesting because going back to that hip-hop debate, someone said that Tupac contradicted himself. When I heard that I said, wait, isn't that the essence of humanity? I feel like Pac perfectly encapsulated what it is to be on a path of enlightenment. It is to embrace yourself on every level and to speak your truth as you understand it at each level. At every level of the way, whatever he was learning, he was connected to, he would take it in, deeply connect it, and then express it through his lens in a way that was service to other people. He was also teaching all of us to explore ourselves. He was teaching all of us how not to fall into this false belief or the mentality of, "I want to be perceived as *this,* so I am going to show only these pieces of me." Pac gave his whole self to the world. How many people can say that? Most people could never. That is what the influence actually is. That was *the* gift for me.

DEVI BROWN
WELLNESS EDUCATOR
ENERGY HEALER
AUTHOR

DERRICK D-NICE JONES

"What Tupac spoke about lyrically, was different compared to everybody else. A lot of this stuff, a lot of the issues he mentioned, people swept under the rug and ignored it. Tupac was loud with it. If it didn't feel right, he spoke his mind about it."

Twenty-twenty was a crazy year. Not just for DJing but for representing our generation of artists and Black executives from my time. I have been self-managed almost my whole career. So, to have this kind of success and do it in an authentic way has been great. I can play any artist I want to in a set and no one will bat an eye. They have come to know I am taking them somewhere with the music. To have the trust of people in this way has been amazing.

My friendship with Tupac was very limited because when he came on the scene it was toward the end of my career as a rap artist. I would see Tupac more during the times he was hanging out with Treach and when I was in Atlanta in the clubs. I would also see him on set, shooting music videos such as the "Doowutchyalike" video. Whenever I saw him, there was mutual respect and love. Treach was my brother and Tupac was his brother, so he always showed love whenever we saw each other. We are both Geminis, which is a different level of understanding. We shared a dedication to our craft and the legacy we want to leave behind.

What's funny is I saw a lot of similarities in the ways Tupac worked, in myself. I put in hours doing things that other people wouldn't do. I don't know anyone that recorded more songs than Tupac in hip-hop. Songs with real lyrics. No disrespect to any current artists, but their lyrics don't read as poetry. Tupac's work was poetry and to me, that's what was brilliant about him. When you read his work, you know poetry was always a part of him. His flow was timeless. You know that you can put any track behind his words, and it still sounds like Tupac. His energy remains and the music still sounds fresh. When you listen to many older artists, it takes you back to their time, but you put a new track under Tupac, and it still sounds fresh. It sounds like he went into the studio last night. That's what was so brilliant about him.

What was so great and so interesting about his activism is that his approach was a lot different than what other MCs of the older generation were doing. Tupac's approach had to do with how he grew up and his mother. His family always represented Black culture. They had a focus on the plight of Black people. His activism stood the test of time. When you listen to those songs now, it's sad to realize we are still going through a lot of the same issues that we experienced when he was making those records thirty years ago. It's beautiful to know that his music was timeless, but it is equally sad to know that we are still dealing with the same challenges. He was willing to speak about it. The only other artist that reminded me of Tupac was DMX. DMX did it in his own way. DMX (RIP) was one of a kind, and Tupac was really one of a kind.

Tupac's activism always felt like the mission was bigger than just him selling records. The mission was bigger than being in the spotlight and taking the credit for anything. It was about the people, and it's beautiful to see that people still celebrate him to this day. People talk about having your brother's back, but I witnessed Tupac being his brother's keeper firsthand, and that is one of my fondest memories I have of him. One day, I watched how he handled my cousin when we were in the club. We were at this club in Atlanta, Georgia, and Tupac was rolling a blunt. He offered it to me, but I hadn't told him I didn't smoke until that night. It was funny because he joked about it with the group, and we laughed. He offered the blunt to my cousin McBoo and suddenly, this flashlight was shining on the two of them. The person says, "You and you, come with me, you're both under arrest." The type of guy Tupac was, he was a stand-up dude. He wasn't going to allow them to arrest my cousin. He told them, "No it was all me; he didn't even touch it; this was on me." They took them both in the back and eventually they arrested

Tupac, but they didn't arrest my cousin because Tupac wouldn't let that happen. So, when you talk about somebody truly being "My Brother's Keeper," that's what Tupac really represents. If you were down with him, he made sure that you were okay, and that's very rare to find, especially at that age and in the hip-hop community. A lot of times people are only looking out for themselves, and he wasn't that way. I will never forget that. Tupac was the truth. The world as well as the hip-hop community was better because of him and the standards he upheld. He was a special individual.

Thug Life wasn't something I saw as gang related. It always felt as though it was calling for Black men to stand up and express that we had enough. Thug Life showed what Black men represent and explained that we're not here for the bullshit. Standing for what we represent, and that is what Thug Life meant to me. This is the energy that I took from it. I always felt like Tupac's mission, even in terms of being a Black man, was always about being the best representation of the way Black men should be. Especially during that time. During that time, when people were taking advantage of Black men, financially. Taking advantage of our crafts, our music, and with the culture in general. Thug Life said, "NO! This is not what we are going to do. This is the change we are looking for." So that's what Thug Life represents to me. I feel like this generation encompasses part of that Thug Life idea. They show that they will stand up for what they believe in and do what needs to be done to see a change in the world.

What Tupac spoke about lyrically, was different compared to everybody else. A lot of the issues he mentioned, people swept under the rug and ignored it. Tupac was loud with it. If it didn't feel right, he spoke his mind about it. Obviously hip-hop and the culture itself shifted and became a lot more glamorous. The videos are focused

127

more on affluence. Everyone started making money and some people lost focus of what that vision was. However, when you fast-forward to where we are now, dealing with what we had to deal with in the past year or two years, where awareness about racial injustice is heightened. Artists have finally started to speak up about it. You see the younger generation, who really are babies, taking a different stance on certain songs. A lot of that "in your face, talking about it" was based on how Tupac was. Tupac was about being in your face and telling you what was wrong. He was about saying *this is what we needed to do to make things right*. Tupac spoke in the language of the average man that was on the streets, dealing with the same struggles. It's very important for that kind of approach to live on because we need it to see change happen.

I wish that I took the opportunity to not be shy and be more open to expressing how I felt for people at the time. Between knowing Tupac and having the chance to work with Prince, I didn't really express how I felt to those icons. I wasn't as vocal as I am now, and I wish that Tupac knew exactly what it was. Tupac was extremely important to me, and he's always been one of my top five favorite MCs ever. It was because lyrically he was just different. I wish I could have been ten percent of the artist and man that he was. I wish I would have been able to express that more, but I know he felt the love from me and everyone around the world. I pray that his legacy lives on.

DERRICK D-NICE JONES
DJ
ARTIST
PRODUCER
PHOTOGRAPHER

DJ TRAUMA

"His music is just so timeless; the things that he was talking about are still relevant. He's just dope!"

THE FIRST TIME I HEARD TUPAC WAS ON "SAME SONG" WITH Digital Underground. The crazy thing was, I didn't know till years later it was Tupac. I think for me, I liked his passion and the way he made you feel with his music. He just had this energy that was unique. It's weird he started off more as an activist, and I feel like he was going back that way when he was killed. For me, being a New Yorker, I had to ride for the home team. I feel like his time was cut short with the activism; he was really getting ready to do big things. What he did do, with all the things he was talking about, was things that needed to be said, and with the compassion he had. I think, also, he was unapologetic, which you hadn't seen at the time. He was so talented, even with his acting, which doesn't get talked about enough, and that is one of his contributions. He wasn't in a box; he was able to explore and be good at all of it. His music is just so timeless; the things that he was talking about are still relevant. He's just dope!

It's weird, because a lot of his music I didn't listen to until he passed, 'cause like I said, when he went at New York, I was like, ehhh, but to go back now, I see why people loved him so much; his lasting effect is so hard to put into words. He is larger than life. Even when he was alive, he already had that legendary status. I just remembered DJing for him when he performed at Clark Atlanta University, and just to get him was an ordeal, 'cause I was a part of the bookings. When he hit that stage, it was crazy. I didn't really understand his impact until I was at a show one day in Atlanta, and you couldn't even move, and the crowd was repeating every word of the song while I'm thinking, "I don't know any of these songs," but that was when I went, "I get it." That show sticks out because even then I'm like, "This is packed," and I didn't hear any promotions, nothing.

131

To me, Thug Life is like a code of the street, and kind of unapologetically you, and loyal to your team, if I had to put it into words. He prepared us for a long road ahead. The moment in time is only a part of the struggle. He was a warrior. I think like all Geminis, Tupac had two sides. His personality could be so calm, which a lot of people did not know.

DJ TRAUMA
DJ

ED LOVER

"He would have moved
mountains for Black people."

IT WAS DIFFERENT FOR ME BECAUSE HE WAS CLOSE TO STRETCH and Stretch's brother Majesty, and DJ K-Low Stretch met Pac on *Juice*. I was in *Juice* for fifteen seconds; if you blink, you'd miss me. What I loved the most about Pac was not only his intelligence, and his ability to sit down, and for us to have an intelligent conversation. He was a lot of fun to be around. When people see Pac, they see Pac one way, but the ones that know him say that he was a lot of fun to be around, and I said the same thing about Biggie. The side of them you don't see is their fun side, their goofy side. Pac was goofy. We always had a good time, but if it came down to his love for Black people, it was always an insightful, intelligent conversation. When he was around us, he wasn't "Tupac," he was Tupac. He was just a really cool guy who was trying to find himself as a man. And people get upset with me when I say that, because I'm telling you the truth about his confusion in life and how afraid he was when he went to jail, and how things changed when he got bailed out. People don't understand, by the time Suge bailed him out, and he was home and he did "California Love," he didn't live a year. We say a lot of things when we are angry or feel betrayed. A lot of things I say at twenty-five are not what I'd say in my fifties, because I'm more mature. So people need to get off the things that Pac said when he was angry. I remember one time, me and Pac got into a scuffle, and he was on this anti-police rant. I said, "Now, you know my brother is a cop," and I go, "Pac, you know all cops ain't bad cops." "Fuck cops, man, all them can go die, every single one of them." "Now, Pac, that's my brother you are talking about." I said, "You say that one more time, and I and you are gonna throw down in this studio." He walked away and said it again. I jumped right on his ass. We tussled on the floor trying to get a heads-up on the other, and Stretch let us go for a minute before breaking us up. So we sat apart from each other, I'm steaming, he was steaming. Fifteen minutes go by and this is how goofy he is, he walked over to me and said, "We smoking or what, nigga?" and we go outside, got some beer, and smoked some blunts like nothing happened. And then later on he apologized.

So what people don't know about Pac is he was so young. When you're that young, you are prone to make mistakes. He's put on such a pedestal, it's hard for people to understand he was a human being. It's hard for people to understand what you think you know is not correct. I told people, I don't look at him the way you'll look at him. He's not what all these people paint... Especially the ones that don't know him, and those are the ones who irk me the most. Not you had an encounter or two or three. Me, Stretch, and Pac, were at the Jack the Rapper convention in Atlanta when the Luke and Dre shit happened. When Luke brought all them boys from Miami, we were right there. It bothers me when people say I was a Pac hater, because there's nobody I love more. I don't even like listening to the song he made with the Outlawz because it came from a place of anger. From a place of someone set me up, and as my man, you should say something. Biggie didn't have that type of power to set you up; he knew nothing. I never knew why Death Row and Bad Boy couldn't coexist, because I knew sooner or later there would have been a Big and Pac album. They would have done something together.

It bothers me that he didn't live to see his potential, 'cause he had so much of it, probably the greatest natural actor I've ever seen in my life. When I look at shows like *The Wire*, I go, "Ah, shit, Pac would have killed that shit." You know, so many movies, because he was that good, and musically his work ethic, the way he wrote, the things he thought about at certain points. The closest thing to Pac is X because both of them, what pulls them and what pulled Pac was, flashy life over here, but my love for my sister and people over here. He's the only person who can make a song about women then (begins singing "Scandalous"). Pac had everything a successful rapper needs, the skillset, the voice, and women loved him. There are only a few people in my career that made me feel like I'm not famous, Tyson, Michael Jordan, Shaq, Ali, and Pac. They changed rooms. There would be people in a room having conversations, but I could see their eyes move. Me, Pac, Stretch, and a bunch of other guys decide to go to the Atlanta "Underground." Now I'm on TV six fucking days a week, I got the number-one-rated show on MTV, and I walk in with people asking for autographs. He came from behind me and it was over. They had to get the police to get us out of there, and I'm like, "I'm famous too."

I don't own a shirt with Tupac's face on it because I don't want to buy it unless it's official. I am so tired of these fucking people who did not know him, didn't love him, media calling him "Two-pack," and now, all of a sudden, every little stand is trying to make money off of him, when before I remember Pac arguing with a Nigerian dude for bootlegging his shit. You selling it is taking away from him getting paid. And now that he died, everyone wants to sell Tupac memorabilia, and attribute quotes to him that he never said. I was on *Clubhouse* one day and someone goes, "Tupac said," and I go, "Tupac said what?" "Oh, in the *Vibe* interview." I go, "Tupac ain't say that shit." I don't think Suge was more like I love this dude, it was more of what can I get out of this dude, or like I'm going to make crazy money on Death Row because now I got Pac. But, being young, I don't think he saw it, 'cause if Pac was with you, he was with you. For us, his agenda was to be self-sufficient; his agenda was for us to open our fucking eyes. Being woke now; he was woke then. He was the son of a group of people who were ostracized and demonized for doing what every white American does. If he was alive now, at fifty, you think he was in the news then. I think because of his Black Panther background, if he saw something, and it was real to him in his heart, he would call it out, and I am sure he would be in the position now, good with money, to say what the fuck he wanted, and at fifty, he'd be a lot calmer. But the fire in his soul for Black people would be strong. He would have been in the position, where I'm speaking and I don't give a fuck. His impact on the youth is wake the fuck up, Black people. He was so beloved, he could have moved mountains. That's what he would be doing at fifty; he would have moved mountains for Black people.

ED LOVER
ENTERTAINER
ACTOR
COMEDIAN
RADIO HOST

FREE MARIE

"Tupac clearly wanted to use his fame to make changes in the community; that part of his story isn't as senstional, so it's not pushed. It's up to us to make sure that the next generation understands how revolutionary he was in his thinking."

WHEN I FIRST SAW TUPAC SHAKUR, HE WAS A PART OF THE group Digital Underground. He was the fine, chocolate, brown-skin brother that came out of what seemed like nowhere on "Same Song." Later on, I would get to know him as Tupac the solo artist. Tupac was what they call wise beyond his years, super aware of the world at a very young age. I can still watch his interviews and catch something I missed or didn't quite understand the first time I listened. He dropped so much knowledge. For goodness' sakes! The man wrote "Dear Mama," (which has to be one of the most vulnerable pieces of art in hip-hop history) at twenty-three years old. TWENTY-THREE years old. At twenty-three, I was going to the club.

He wrote "Brenda's Got a Baby" years before that, and I remember thinking, damn, is he on my block? Here was a young Black man, telling young Black women, me, us...that everything was gonna be alright and to keep our heads up. He had us all right then and there, yet, at the same time, he was Thug Life-ing and telling stories the hood could relate to. This...was Tupac's genius.

If you listen to the messages in his music and watch some old interviews about his views on education, civil rights, and oppression, you would understand what was in his heart, what fueled his passions. That is why, in my opinion, he inspired so many. Young, vulnerable, outspoken, vivid, talented, hungry, crazy, and empowered. He was a thinker, sharing his plans and thoughts about education and observations on society, but at the same time, he was the man we saw talking all that shit; he was Thug Life.

When I listen to Pac, he inspires me to be fearless and outspoken; he reminds me that we all have a part to do in this place, while we are here. At other times, during certain songs, he also inspires me to get my Thug Life on, energy transfers, and every time you hear Tupac, that's that energy coming for ya. It is what it is. Tupac never apologized for being who he was at his core, at his best nor at his worst. He was also honest with himself. He knew he couldn't fix the world but that he would be an inspiration for someone who would.

Tupac clearly wanted to use his fame to make changes in the community; that part of his story isn't as sensational, so it's not pushed. It's up to us to make sure that the next generation understands how revolutionary he was in his thinking, how young he was when he made an impact, and how important and relevant his ideas were. In such a short time, he impacted so many people, so many hearts, so many kids. So I hope we keep telling his story, sharing his quotes and passion for a better world. That's all.

RIP Tupac Shakur

A personal memory:

I remember when Tupac's documentary came out in 2003, while I was hosting *106 & Park*. I was invited by Afeni Shakur to watch the documentary with her, (her daughter) Set Shakur (who he mentions in his "Dear Mama" song), and a few family members. I was so honored to be there. It was also the first time either had seen it, so it wasn't an easy task. For years I looked back on that day and kicked myself for not asking to interview Afeni Shakur...(At the time, I didn't want to overstep my welcome). Now I understand that every moment isn't meant for the rest of the world, so I stopped kicking myself and now I cherish this memory. RIP Queen Afeni and Prince Pac.

May your legacy live on through your family and The Tupac Amaru Shakur Foundation.

FREE MARIE
HIP HOP JOURNALIST
PHILANTHROPIST
ENTREPRENEUR
PRODUCER

GRACE HARRY

"It was clear that Tupac had gifts greater and more complex than what our community currently had the tools or the foundation to support to its full luminosity. And that magnitude of energy is hard to hold up on your own."

990, I AM WATCHING MTV AND A DIGITAL UNDERGROUND VIDEO CAME on. I am immediately blown away by the energy of one. I was fixated on Tupac Amaru Shakur. The more I learned about him, the more I was interested. I was 20 years old and I had not experienced many men, especially Black men, who were able to live in the duality of their vulnerability and their strength to survive. It was clear that Tupac had gifts greater and more complex than what our community currently had the tools or the foundation to support to its full luminosity. And that magnitude of energy is hard to hold up on your own.

Two years later, I would have the privilege of working with him directly on Juice. I was the publicity assistant at MCA records. I was asked to cover a press conference with the actors of The movie. Connecting with him was so impressive. He walked into each interview with the full embodiment of his character, leaving Tupac in the green room. It sounds like a simple thing but in my 31 years working with many artists, I know it is not. Actors are taught to release who they think they are and embody a character. Recording artists are taught to create or at least magnify a larger than life "always" character to connect to the music's experience. Letting go of all the things you walk around the world believing represent you and your success is challenging. You have to be willing to be inside this other experience so you can sell it and sympathize with that character.

Tupac stacked on top of all of that raw emotion and creative energy, a salve to receive the world's truth for us to take our own version of action. Often artists get penalized for taking their music into a political space or picking a position. He did it in such a sexy and effortless way, taking very complicated situations and framing them in a way where you felt and empathized.

GRACE HARRY
JOY STRATEGIST

147

GRAND PUBA

"With his vision, knowing him, how he moved and his energy, his vision was, don't talk about it; be about it. In order to be successful in what we need to accomplish as a people, that is what we need to do; we need to be about it and not just talk about it."

I WILL TAKE IT FROM THE BEGINNING OF HOW WE INTERTWINED and how we connected; it starts with my uncle (Ahmed Obafemi), and my aunt (Fulani sunni-Ali). In the struggle fighting for freedom, land, and independence. As kids, we were subjected and brought into that awareness, into our history, who we are, what we are fighting for—basically the struggle. On Malcolm X's birthday, we would drive to the gravesite and put flowers there. They would give demonstrations; we were in the Black Power movement with several organizations throughout the years. There was the Black Panther Party, the Republic of New Afrika, the New African People's Organization, etc. As I got older, I got into the rap game. We had a meeting at my aunt's house, with some of my cousins and several other people. The meeting was about what the struggle was, what the organization was, and who would do what. They were bringing us into the situation. I said to your dad, "I do music and I love music." However, I am with it in whatever way I can be a part of, I'm definitely for the liberation of our people, count me in. If I can go through the music, so be it. On the first Brand Nubian record, the title for the album was the song. I mentioned in a line there, "A Wisdom to me is someone like Assata, Peace to T'Khikuma, Ahmed, and Kenyatta, brothers that'll fight for the cause." If you go back and listen, this is around the same time and setting when we had the meeting. I told Unc that I am with it 100 percent.

Moving forward, to the '90s, I had to perform on *The Arsenio Hall Show* and *In Living Color* out in LA. We arrived at LAX; Pac is there. We were at the baggage claim. I spoke to him. He said, "They told me you were coming; I got you while you're out here." I didn't figure it out until later, but people in the movement may have told him I was coming. He took us to eat at Roscoe's Chicken and Waffles. He had a brand-new black Benz with the paper tags in the window. There were a couple of cars and about eight or nine of us. He had people with him as well. As we were getting ready to get into the car, Pac said, "Whoever is riding in this car, if the police pull us over, I'm not getting on the ground. If you plan on getting on the ground if the police pull us over, you need to ride in another car." My only felony was an assault on the police chief, other than my juvie stuff, so I am thinking how I am not getting on the ground either. I sat in the back and Jay sat in the front. I'm in the back and between the passenger seat and back seat was a wooden chest/box. I lifted it and he had about five or six handguns in the box. Now I see why we wouldn't be getting on the ground. If this is what it is, then this is what it is.

We went to eat and afterward I had a show. If you go to YouTube and look up Grand Puba, Tupac, and Treach, that was the same night. The show was great. We were backstage freestyling with some guys from Compton videotaping everything. When we finished, we went out to the front of the party and there was some commotion going on involving one of my dancers and one of the locals. I look at Pac and tell him we may have an issue here. He bolts out of the door; automatically I remembered what he had in the car. I knew what he was going to do. By the time he went out and came back, everything was squashed and good. He came in turned-up. I had to tell him we were good and we decided to get out of there. We went back to the hotel. The next day I had to do Arsenio; at ten a.m., he knocked on my door. I open the door and he hands me a Glock, cocked, one in the chamber, and the clip was in his other hand. He told me to hold onto it while I was in LA. I haven't wiped the rocks out of my eyes. I was holding the Glock thinking, "This is crazy." I ended up doing the Arsenio show. There was a lot of love. That night, there was an event going on after, on Sunset at The Comedy Store. Eddie Griffin was slated to be there. I felt like it was time to handle the rest of my business and get out of there.

152

The next day I had to do *In Living Color* and Pac came with us on set. I had to be there at ten in the morning. We were drinking 40s and smoking. They had us sit there while they filmed the whole season's episodes. We were there until two in the morning to do one song. Everyone was cool, though. We met Jamie and J-Lo. We didn't meet anyone from the Wayans family. We were there for about four hours. As we were leaving and walking to the limo, the pizza delivery guy was coming with ten pies. Pac said, "Those are coming with us. All of the ones without pepperoni are going with us." We took all of the food. Years later I'm in this club and this is the same place we had that issue. I see Damon from *My Wife and Kids*, he walks up to me and says, "So you got the pizza, huh?" I died laughing because this was years later. We all laughed it off and joked about it. There are so many stories, and we did a lot together. Whenever events were done in the movement, they called two people for fundraisers or whatever it was they needed, me and Pac. We were doing an event for the New Black Panther Party in Tougaloo, Mississippi, while he was also shooting *Above the Rim*. I got there first and he arrived. It looked as if the Civil Rights Movement was back in Tougaloo. Everything in Tougaloo looks nostalgic. I did my soundcheck, and Pac does his. As he was doing his soundcheck, a drunk dude was in the bleachers watching. He yelled, "Hey, Mr. Tupac." I'm saying to myself, "Oh boy," because I already know. He does not understand that all of Pac's people are behind him while he is taunting Pac. Pac was telling him to chill and he wanted to just do his soundcheck. The dude is like, "I want to hear what Mr. Tupac has to say." Pac tells him, "You aren't going to hear me; you will feel me."

His music was soldier music. His music was revolutionary music to fight a revolutionary war. Not just right on and keep it moving. There is footage from Africa where the rebel soldiers had Tupac

T-shirts with his picture on them as part of their army uniform. I forgot what tribe it was or who they were fighting. Their uniform was Tupac T-shirts, and I thought, you can't get more revolutionary than that. These kids were young at thirteen, fourteen years old fighting the civil war. There was another time we were talking and he said, "I don't like my voice." I told him to stop doubling his voice, and it sounded clearer when he did not. I told him that he had a dope voice and to trust me. In the song, "I Get Around" and "Dear Mama," you can tell he changed, and it sounded good.

Thug Life is knowing what the problems are in our society, such as us as a people, nation, community, and what we are going through. Being able to handle it and deal with it and to find some way out. To come out of that condition and not be stuck in it.

With his vision, knowing him, how he moved and his energy, his vision was, "Don't talk about it; be about it." In order to be successful in what we need to accomplish as a people, that is what we need to do. We need to be about it and not just talk about it. That was how he moved; he was a little hot-headed at times but loyal. If he is riding, he is riding. His vision was, if it is time to ride, there is no time to talk about it; we have to be about it.

GRAND PUBA
MASTER OF CEREMONY

JAY DIXON

"Tupac's contribution to me and the majority of us is to live in truth, go every day as hard as you can, whether people accept you or not, and be willing to live with your choice."

YOU'VE HEARD 90,000 RAPPERS; ALL OF THE YOUNG ONES SAY THEY have a little Tupac in them. His contribution to them was obviously an idol kind of thing. Their freedom of speech or recklessness was his contribution to them. Tupac's contribution to me and the majority of us is to live in truth, go every day as hard as you can, whether people accept you or not, and be willing to live with your choice.

We were with Grand Puba in LA doing *The Arsenio Hall Show* and *Soul Train*. Me, DJ Alamo, Treach from Naughty by Nature, and Tupac went to a comedy show around the time Eddie Griffin started to blow up. We walked in and took a seat. We were excited because the girl in the "Rump Shaker" video with the saxophone was there. Eddie Griffin was there killing it. This drug dealer walked in and said, "What's up, Pac?" shaking his hand. He proceeded to order shots and champagne and sent them to our section. There are seventy-five shots of Hennessy and seventy-five bottles of champagne for the four of us and him. Pac, being the person he is, is shaking his hand back. I'm thinking of free drinks. Pac orders seventy-five shots of Hennessy and seventy-five bottles of champagne and sends it to him. In the middle of all of this, we are trying to drink seventy-five bottles of champagne and Hennessy. We are lit and Eddie Griffin is on the stage. All of a sudden, we heard rumblings and a crew of people walked in. Some Crips walked in and one barked orders, telling them where to go. When I looked up, no one was at the table. I looked down to see Pac and Alamo and unconsciously dove on the ground still holding a drink. We were on the floor face to face, still drinking our drinks, saying, "They are going to kill us tonight, so try to finish these seventy-five bottles of champagne and seventy-five shots of Hennessy." We left out of the comedy club on Sunset

Boulevard; throughout all of that, Pac and I still had a bottle of champagne and a shot of Hennessy.

I had a young rapper named Pumpkin Head who I took to meet Tupac. He was fifteen years old, dumbfounded; his eyes were huge, looking at us everywhere we went that night. While we were talking, Tupac said he needed to go to the studio to do a verse with Freddy Foxx. Myself, Tupac, and Pumpkin Head drove to Queens. We arrived and banged on the door wondering why no one was answering. Pumpkin Head was imitating Tupac. If Tupac moved two steps another way, he moved two steps that way. He was trying to touch Tupac's shoulders. Meanwhile, we are still banging on the door when finally, Freddy Foxx comes to the door holding two machetes. So Pac pulls out two guns and says, "It's me." When we walked in, the first person he saw was Benzino in a hockey jersey from Boston.

Tupac's vision prepared us for the world today because he called it. Everything that is going on, he called it. We were raised like that, from Freedom Group to Thug Life to everything being talked about is everything he called. Thug Life to me represents the freedom to be aggressive. This is based on everything we learned since our youth.

JAY DIXON
ENTERTAINMENT MANAGER
FAMILY MEMBER

JEFF DIXON

"Thug Life was him agitating the community. When I hear Thug Life, it means to not compromise who I am."

TUPAC'S MUSIC MADE PEOPLE KEEP IT REAL. THE YOUTH WHO didn't know how to translate it. How to translate that realness. His music started making people say, "Man, I can go with that, and I come with that type of energy," and I think it was confusing to a lot of the youth at first; they were like, he's talking one way but I don't see it, because we never heard it this raw. On a national level, 'cuz coming from Interscope, you might hear things, but coming the way he came, with the movement, it made people wanna be like, man, I kinda gotta learn more about my history or see where he is coming from in that perspective...

When I first heard the lyrics, being from New York and familiar with lyrics that were deep and conscious, it didn't really affect me because I was used to it. It was when he went deeper in certain topics and the passion behind it. You had certain people and groups that would touch on those topics, but no one did it like Pac. He made you think, and him coming from that West Coast perspective, you saw he had something to say.

Just him holding it down. It's funny, because the whole crew were on the West Coast, and as soon as we got there, he met us at this hotel. I don't remember the name of it, but I remember that it had this kitchen in the room. As soon as we got there, we let him know that we were there. He says to us, "Yo, y'all here. I got y'all." When he showed up, he pulled out a bag of guns and proceeded to tell us what we needed and for what. The guns were everywhere, taking up each inch of this hotel room. He gave us a tutorial of what we needed to do, including how to dance and the colors we shouldn't wear. Us being from New York, we thought what real was, but he let us know what real was on that side. He was basically our tour guide. He told us that when we got stopped (by who) he wasn't getting the...(can't hear what he says is not being retrieved when they get stopped). Immediately, my flags went up. That wasn't my kind of vibe. Puba and I were always different, in the way that we moved. Jay and the others were always down for any and everything. They rode around smoking in the new Benz, driving through Hollywood. For me, it didn't make any sense, because, me being used to how it was in New York, I just knew they would get stopped.

He kept us in the loop about the situation that occurred with LL, where he almost got snatched off stage because of his colors. With that happening and Pac looking out for us knowing that we were family, and him wanting to make sure we were good, was nothing short of respect and appreciation. This is a story I will never forget. That night we also went out to a comedy club because we wanted to go out and have a good time. When we got there, there was a whole table full of alcohol, and everyone else was already enjoying themselves. Puba and I came in afterwards. We moved slow, and when we got there, it must have been just as the peak of when things really started to get exciting. There was one guy there, I don't remember exactly which gang he was affiliated with, but what I do remember is, all hell broke loose. We saw the young homies coming in as we were in the lobby leaving out. We saw DOC and he let us know what was going down. We just started seeing people running out the lobby and jumped over "the thing." I said to him, "Yo, cousin, let's get up outta here."

As everyone was leaving, Snoop Dogg and others showed up and they greeted Puba and (Pac) and we all went back to the hotel and ate bologna sandwiches and hung out. We did a rhyming session as well. The crazy thing is, Snoop didn't actually like Pac that much at the time. So, we were all in the room, doing a rhyming session, and Snoop took one gun out of his right-side pocket and slammed it on the table, and then he took another gun out of his left-side pocket and slammed it on the table, and he started rhyming. I remember looking at Pac like, yo, this dude is crazy. I always felt that he was misunderstood. He was very passionate, but that wasn't understood by most.

Thug Life was him agitating the community. When I hear Thug Life, it means to not compromise who I am. You have to accept me for who I am because I'm going to get it either way. That was the mindset of the young people in our time. We were going to make it by any means necessary. It was that Malcom X mentality. That's what Tupac was about, and he said it in his way. Thug Life is about us thuggin' through. Whatever we had to do to get what we wanted. That mentality we had on the block. We stayed out here all day, until we got this little bit of money, because we weren't going to be broke for the rest of our lives.

JEFF DIXON
CO-CEO OF EBONY SON ENTERTAINMENT
CO-CEO OF DISTURBING THA PEACE

KAINON JASPER

"Tupac was very young, and if he had the opportunity to mature to what that kind of warrior class makes you, then I believe things would have been different. They would have been a whole lot different because of his ability to call people out with the range and material he had. He was very courageous."

FIRST TIME I WAS INTRODUCED TO TUPAC WAS DURING DIGITAL Underground, through "Same Song." I immediately paid attention to the African references because of how I was raised and how we were raised. So that immediately caught my eyes. I noticed his smile was so big, and his name, "Tupac," was different, and it made a statement. From there I wanted to know more about who he was and his music. Digital Underground was also hot and refreshing and fun.

I think as far as the range and effect, no one else has what he has. Nobody. Now, I saw a bit of range in artists such as LL COOL J, but Tupac was different. He was like the toughest dudes in the world rocked with him. In this day and age, they still reference him. Decades later, we still hear them reference his lyrics with the same fervor as if he wrote them yesterday. Certain tattoo placements and demeanor, nobody has impacted on that kind of range. Tupac made you think. He spoke to all of the emotions. His long-lasting effects are in the ability to look at ourselves with imperfections. Rap music is very interesting if it is used the right way. You hear certain people say certain things and Tupac, he addressed imperfections. Lyrics such as, "Even though you were a crack fiend, Mama, you always was a Black queen, Mama." How dare you say that with such truth and so much love? He brought the emotion out, and you now see people rap with so much emotion and vulnerability. He definitely impacted me from that perspective. Even from the start, with songs such as "Brenda Got a Baby." You felt bad. From the standpoint of becoming more emotional, the impact definitely belongs to him.

I met Tupac through my cousin Bryce who was in Groove Theory at the time. Now, I am very particular about people, because you can see something on the outside and yet what's going on in their mind is very different. People don't know who I am behind what they see. They don't know my Pan-African background. They don't know how I like to read and my thirst for knowledge. I can give and participate with a certain group of people who grew up similar to myself and my family. Good, bad, or indifferent. That's what it was. A lot of people were unaware of what was going on in my head and the heads of those like me. When I met Tupac, his energy was crazy. He was so excited, and it made me really look at him and as if he was on something. Generally, we were cool, but he was so excited naturally. He reminded me of a dude who was from the South who came to New York for the first time. That was the kind of energy he had. I remember we went to the club, and this was after *Juice* came out. We were in the club and there was this girl looking at him. He said, "Yo, that's the same girl I was trying to kick it with last year and she wouldn't give me the time of day. Now, she won't stay outta my face." She kept coming over and he was curving her, and then her girlfriend came over and said that her friend really wants to meet him. He said something to her and dismissed her. However, there was a lady in the wheelchair and he actually ended up dancing with the lady in the wheelchair. He danced with her for what seemed like an hour. The lady was so happy. He was turning her around and sincerely helping this woman have a good time and having a good time himself. I just observed in amazement because two minutes ago, he was talking to me about some crazy things, and then, five minutes later, he was making someone's world change. Then, he came back and started talking about our responsibility as Black men. In my head I'm like, "Woah, you were just three different people in five minutes." That's the type of person I remember. Those are the stories I have. He had range, and though I wasn't aware of what it was back then, I knew he was electric. It struck me because my cousin said we were going to get along just fine and we did. It was so unexpected and I didn't know him *that* well, but the way I was introduced to him, there was no filter. He already trusted me based on what he was told I was, and there was no doubt in my mind that if that day we were in that club and a fight broke out, he was fighting right there with me. He was also very complimentary of people. He wasn't shy of telling people that they had a great vibe, handsome, pretty, none of that.

Thug Life wasn't something I actually liked that much. I saw the other part of Tupac, and when it came to Thug Life, I saw the misinterpretations of it. When he was in New York, some of the people we knew mutually, were being misinterpreted. A lot of guys who are outcasted, don't want to be outcasted. If they could choose to be in a different world, another world, and be accepted, they would. Don't let some of their circumstances and what you see, make you think that is their mentality. Some of these guys are very bright and had little to no options early on, and there are also cultural factors. I thought he misinterpreted and he saw the outside and thought that he could morph into that, but what I felt like he didn't understand was that these guys were who they were from years of being taught how to behave that way, given the circumstances. It's not something that you just wear. Most of the guys you are looking at thinking they were tough gangsta guys were actually very calm and charismatic. Thug Life revved up an engine that came with a lot of circumstances. I had an opportunity to speak to him about it once, but I believe he was too far up the momentum. He received it and tried to explain that Thug Life wasn't about being a street guy or a gangster, but I expressed that the things surrounding him said something different to a lot of cats who are unable to interpret it that way. So, I moved away from the Thug Life vibe.

I think if we bought into Tupac's vision a bit more, we would be much more prepared. We would protect our women a little bit more. We would have a lot more self-love as far as being Black people. African people. His vision was to be more educated, prepared, and equipped. Know who you are and know some historical data that you can apply to certain things. As well as how to be unapologetically you. Being a Black person, growing up under these circumstances, at times you have to be unapologetic. Not disrespectful, but claim your place in this word and understand that. Black people in this world are always taking a shape in a political and cultural movement. We have always done that. If we can align ourselves with other groups that share the same mentality so that the fight isn't happening with just one individual but as a group. The support becomes a group effort. I don't think we could see it at the time, and some people who claimed to be down or about Tupac, didn't truly continue the work. Doesn't seem like they were really listening, because if they were, then a chain wouldn't be so important. Certain European clothing wouldn't be so important. The treatment of our own people would be a lot different. Tupac was very young, and if he had the opportunity to mature to what that kind of warrior class makes you, then I believe things would have been different. They would have been a whole lot different because of his ability to call people out with the range and material he had. He was very courageous.

We can all play his music a lot more and find a new perspective. With me being fifty-one now, I have a completely different perspective than I had back then. A lot of things I believe we should revisit. I listened to a Stevie Wonder song the other day, "As," and this was a song I know by heart, ad libs and all. However, just the other day, I noticed that the song said something that I didn't pay attention to before. Someone like Tupac has a lot of those deeper/hidden messages in his music that can be dissected today.

KAINON JASPER
BRIDGE INTELLIGENCE GROUP/PRINCIPAL

KELLY L. JACKSON

"His music will never die, his poetry will never die, it's like those special collections of books we have, you can pick it up anytime, anywhere, and still feel connected to him, so it's the connectivity he has with us forever."

BEING A LOVER OF HIP-HOP, I AM FROM THE MIDWEST, FLINT, Michigan, so we get the best of both worlds. There was something special about Tupac. I loved Tupac because it felt different. I am a lover of handsome men, so, first, he was fine with me, and then his lyrics. His lyrics were so beautiful, like "Brenda's got a baby," because it connects with you. There are so many stories in the ghettos and the streets of children who have that story. He had substance; what he was talking about was stuff we were living and seeing, and it made him stand out to me. Tupac is the father of so many children who are lovers of music. There's always a song that we can go back to that he left us. I always felt he died at a young age but did so much. I think for hip-hop and the culture, he could be viewed in the same light as King (MLK). I worked at StepSun Music, and one of my first projects was working with the late, great Paul Mooney on his comedy albums, *Race* and *Master Piece*. I found out Tupac loved Paul Mooney. I was at the Jack the Rapper convention and saw Tupac coming up the escalator and I knew I had to do something. I stood in front of him, introduced myself, and told him that I worked with Paul Mooney and how I could send him his albums. Tupac told me how to get the albums to him and I did just that. The albums were great collections.

I eventually saw him a few months later in New York, and I'll never forget it. I went up to him and said, "I'm Kelly; I'm the person who sent you the albums." His eyes lit up, and in my world, it was just me and him. He gave me this big hug and said, "That was you! Thank you," then we had a small conversation. It took all I had to stay calm and composed. Another time, I lost my Sky Pager because of Tupac. Tupac introduced Biggie at a CMJ convention in New York, "I Get Around" plays, my hands went in the air, my pager went somewhere, even though I needed it, because all my contacts were

175

in there, it didn't matter, that was my connection to Tupac. There was something about his energy being so genuine for me, and that small time frame I was able to meet him, I'll always remember it. His music and poetry are an evergreen vibe. His music will never die, his poetry will never die, it's like those special collections of books we have, you can pick it up anytime, anywhere, and still feel connected to him, so it's the connectivity he has with us forever. He was just this spirit that was meant for the time and purpose because of the things he said when he was living. You know the times we're in now, we talk about police brutality, he was talking about that then. So when we look at George Floyd and all the others, Tupac was talking about injustice, inequality. Tupac's case with the police, that was big; think about how it was taken by the press, it started small but it became bigger. He used his voice to highlight it. It shined a light for all to embrace forever!

KELLY L. JACKSON
EXECUTIVE

KEVIN POWELL

"I've been to places where I've met people who weren't even born in 1996, who said they love Tupac Shakur. I ask why and they say because he taught me not to be scared."

I'VE BEEN A CIVIL AND HUMAN RIGHTS ACTIVIST SINCE I WAS A youth in the 1980s. I started in activism because of the anti-apartheid movement, because of elder activists like Kwame Ture and Ahmed Obafemi. These were names that were shared with me as a teenager and were a big part of my conscious development. I also grew up a hip-hop head, so as I was becoming conscious, or woke, as we say now, I was learning stuff that I didn't know growing up. It's such a blessing for people like you, Aiyisha, Tupac, and Set, who had parents who were in the movement, because you all got a history and education that many of us did not get. I crammed once I started reading and learning, and I felt like I had to learn about the '60s and '70s, and I learned of all these names, such as Ture, Shakur, Obafemi, Lumumba, and I began to realize not only was there a civil rights movement, but there was a Black power, Black social movement that I was not aware of. Once I did become aware, I became deeply involved in it as a youth. As I was also popping and locking and breakdancing and deeply involved in hip-hop as well. I went to school at Rutgers in New Jersey because I was born and raised in Jersey City, and the irony of all this is that I met a lot of people in Jersey who were part of the movement, such as Sister Souljah when she was still Lisa Williamson and the Baraka family, including Ras Baraka and his father, the late Amiri Baraka. It was just an incredible time to be a young person in the '80s and '90s when you look back on it because there's a lot of deep stuff happening.

While there were still a lot of attacks on our people and activists who were revolutionaries, it was also this revolutionary culture we were coming into. By the time I started to hear the changes in our music with people like Queen Latifah and Public Enemy with Chuck D, we began to feel like this is our culture and we were saying stuff just like the Last Poets did, just like Bob Marley and Nina Simone did. I always told myself that I wanted to be a journalist because I wanted to tell the stories of our people that were left out of the mainstream media. A lot of the stuff I did in the beginning of my career was centered around African American news and Caribbean news, because wherever our people were, I wanted to tell our stories. In 1990 an interesting thing happened during the time I moved to New York City from Jersey City. A brother, Harry Allen, who Chuck D talked about on the Public Enemy song "Don't Believe the Hype," who is considered the father of hip-hop journalism, asked me if I ever wrote about hip-hop, and I lied and said yeah, I had. I was just trying to get that check. I was just out here hustling and trying to make it happen because I was now living in New York, and I had to make things happen. So, I started writing about hip-hop and reading stuff, and this was before *The Source* and *Vibe* magazine and all the things that came after it. I just felt like when I was reading about hip-hop, it was by people who were outside of the culture, outside of the community. So that's how it started for me, so from 1990 to 1992, I just started writing as much as I could. I was still doing news reporting for different newspapers such as *The Amsterdam News* out in Harlem. However, I also started to write about our culture as an insider. Someone who is actually Black. It was around that time that I first began to hear about Tupac Shakur, but I didn't make the connection then.

I saw the name Tupac and I heard Shakur and, as I said earlier, Shakur, just like Obafemi and Baraka, are royalty to us who are in the movement. Individuals such as myself, who didn't grow up with father figures, these individuals and these families meant a lot to us. I remember my four years at Rutgers University—and for about three or four years—Kwame Ture would come to speak. We just kept bringing him back. We were young and hungry for knowledge and wanted to connect to people, to history. We just wanted to learn. I remember me and a Puerto Rican brother poet—because I was also writing poetry around this time, were in a cafe in Manhattan. It was Tony Medina from the Bronx, and he was telling me about this movie called *Juice*. I remember that we went to see it in Washington Heights, and they had metal detectors and dogs, yet there really wasn't anyone there. I asked myself, "What are all these metal detectors and dogs here for?" So, with it being so much nonsense back then, and this was a movie about young Black males, Black youth, it was assumed some kind of violence was going to happen. Yet there was nothing like that. I remember sitting in that theater and I was blown away by Tupac Shakur and his performance. I was just like, "Who is this dude?" The other brothers in the movie were dope, but it was something about Tupac's spirit that just hit me. I finally connected the dots, and I was like, "Oh, the rapper 2Pac is Tupac Shakur! This is the same dude!" So, within a couple of months after I'm picked to be on the first season of MTV's *The Real World* and we started shooting in February of 1992. What Tupac didn't know is that Quincy Jones at the same time had started putting together *Vibe* magazine. I got an opportunity to do a review for the first issue of *Vibe* and it was on Grand Puba and his solo album. I was so happy because anything Quincy Jones did, I wanted to be in. I wanted to be in this magazine, though I didn't know what it was going to be. The editor-in-chief, Jonathan Van Meter, read something that I wrote on being a young Black man in America. At that time, I was definitely that cat who made it his duty to make everything I was going to write about what we have to go through. How we have to survive. So Jonathan said to me, "Would you like to do a bigger article?" And I said, "Yeah, sure." I didn't know what it was going to be. I ended up doing the cover story on rap supergroup Naughty by Nature for the very first issue. I didn't know that Treach and Tupac were close friends as I was writing that Naughty by Nature cover story.

I wrote the article, but it was hard to write it because Treach was a young Black man trying to figure out how to make it through life. His song "Ghetto Bastard" had especially hit me hard. That first *Vibe* issue with Treach on the cover with his shirt off, to me all of that, was beautiful, because dark-skinned Black people were rarely portrayed properly in the media; everything was about light skin. I thought it was so beautiful what we were doing. The magazine sold out in September 1992. Months earlier, in May 1992, my MTV show, *The Real World*, became the first major reality television show. I didn't know what it was going to be, and I didn't realize how big it was until we went to the Video Music Awards in September '92 in Los Angeles and people were screaming for us like we were Michael Jackson or the Beatles. It was bananas for the seven of us. Little did I know at the time that Tupac Shakur had been watching my season of the show. I found out a year later. *Vibe* became official and Quincy Jones got the green light for his partnership with Time Inc. to publish the magazine fully. We were going to launch it in September of 1993. I'm thinking, okay, great, now I got to get ready. And what I was doing was gathering every article I could find about the history of the Black Power Movement, and the Black Liberation Movement, about the Shakur family, because I knew that I wanted to write about Tupac Shakur.

When they told me I could write about anything, I felt that at that point I had to write about Tupac. First, he represented this intersection between Public Enemy and N.W.A. He had this ability to speak to all sides of our communities, and I didn't think that anyone else could do this. At the same time, Pac was only twenty-one, twenty-two years old. I will never forget it: in March of 1993 we had our first *Vibe* staff meeting. Everyone was pitching what they wanted to write about. One writer decided to write about Rastafarian culture in Jamaica. Another said they wanted to write about Bobby Brown. Then they got to me, and I had a stack of Tupac stuff. I did all this research and I told them I wanted to write about Tupac Shakur, and I was explaining to them this is who he is. I explained to them that I thought he was the James Dean of our generation. At the end of my pitch, they just looked at me, still questioning who he was, and I was like, "Wow." This is supposed to be a magazine for urban culture, for hip-hop, for Black culture. Black people. Black males. And you don't know who Tupac Shakur is? They decided that I was going to write about Snoop Dogg. So, the next cover ended up being on Snoop Dogg.

In the summer of '93, on assignment to write about Snoop, a few colleagues and I were sent to the Jack the Rapper music conference in Atlanta. One of the individuals I was with was Karla Radford, who ended up being our special events director at *Vibe* for many years. We were in the lobby of this conference hotel and there was this huge crowd of people around somebody, but we didn't know who it was. Karla found out it was Tupac and told me to go talk to him. I was scared because he was famous. I wasn't thinking to myself that I had just been on the first season of a famous reality show, or how Quincy Jones was saying my name all over TV. I never thought like that. I was always the young cat who was the writer, not the upfront cat. That's not who I was. I wanted to tell the stories. I was shy and introverted. But Karla goes over there, this little woman, and taps Tupac on the shoulder and says, "Yo, Tupac, you need to know Kevin Powell. He's a writer and he's going to write about you for *Vibe* magazine." Tupac pivots and goes, "Yo, dog! I watched you on that show!" He was so excited to meet me. That day, I realized that he was a fan of mine, and I was a fan of his. It blew my mind. That's how the friendship started. That first sit-down, he says to me, "I want you to be Alex Haley to my Malcolm X." I thought that was incredibly bold and I thought, "Well, what if I want to be Malcolm too?" That's how it all began: 1993 to 1996. I was with Tupac in Atlanta. I was with Tupac in Los Angeles and in New York, and when he went to jail in New York, and I was in Vegas when he died. It became a journey. I thought it was going to be one article, but it turned into a three-year journey that has turned into nearly thirty years of studying his life and art.

I felt like one of Tupac's protectors. I felt like that when he was alive, and I felt like that even after he passed away. I feel like I have a responsibility because it's not just protecting Pac; it is about protecting our families and the activist families that I named before. It's not just about hip-hop. It's bigger than hip-hop. It was so deep for me. I realized I never intentionally took a photo with Tupac. But there's a photo of Afeni Shakur and Tupac walking in court, one of the New York courts, and the picture shows I'm walking behind them. It's deep. People don't understand the whirlwind that it was. What people do not understand is that Pac is loved by millions of people around the world, but there's such a small circle that actually knew him. I'm one of those people, and I don't take that for granted. Since Pac died, I've gone through two bankruptcies, divorces, having money, not having money, and I still keep the tapes of the interviews we did. They are sacred to me. In the famous prison interview, he says to me, I didn't do that to that young lady. Then Pac said what he was responsible for was not stopping the guys around him from hurting that young lady. I have used that in conversations with young men about manhood, about how Pac took responsibility for his associations. At that time, he was still only twenty-three years old, but there was so much happening. It was the situation in Atlanta where they lied and said he rolled up on police, and it's like no, he didn't roll up on police, he was defending someone like a superhero. It's hard because these articles would try to dehumanize him, and yet when I interviewed him, I focused on humanizing him every step of the way because this is a Black man, and he was a famous, young Black man. It wasn't as if he was getting a blueprint for how to deal with it. On top of that, he comes from a political family who also went through a lot.

The Kevin Powell that Pac saw on *The Real World*, that he connected with and trusted, is the Kevin Powell that was raised by our political activists and political movements. So, there was a trust there because he realized I was one of his people. I was part of the tribe. I already knew he was one of my people. People who are not in our tribe, do not understand that. People do not understand what it is like to be a movement child. It's fashionable now to have an Islamic or African name, but growing up, those names were dissed, out of our ignorance. Pac described it as being Black hippies, but he and his family were teaching us how to love ourselves as Black people. That is what was permeating throughout his music.

I was upset when the verdict came out and Pac was sent to jail. I felt that Pac was targeted in so many ways. I remember being at *Vibe* magazine while he was at Rikers Island, and a colleague said to me that Interscope sent over the record they were going to put out, and it was "Dear Mama." I cried. I cried for Afeni Shakur, and I cried for Tupac. I prayed for his life, that he would be okay. I just remember for me personally, who was raised by a strong Black woman in a Black-woman-led family—I just cried so much over that song. There was no way that someone could write a song like this and do what he was accused of doing. There was no way that someone could be reaching to the depth of their own feminine energy and do something like this. In the song, he says "Even as a crack fiend, Mama/You always was a Black queen, Mama." That just tore at me. That tells me that there's a level of empathy and compassion that this man has for what this woman has been through. I don't play this song a lot, but I play it when I need to hear his voice when I'm writing. I play it when I need to think about Ms. Shakur. I play it when I need to think about my mother and how important she is to me. There are moments that Tupac had musically, like "Keep Ya Head Up," "Dear Mama," "Life Goes On." I feel that "Life Goes On" is one of his most underrated songs. I often look at the cover story of the prison interview—it is framed on my wall—and he says that I want people to have the whole story in case I don't make it.

When you think about the fact that he was on MTV, and he talked about Donald Trump in 1992. He saw what was going on way before a lot of us. I feel like his work predicted Black Lives Matter. I feel like "Keep Your Head Up" predicted the #MeToo movement. He was fearless. There was an energy about him that was refreshing. I'm not one of those cats to get sensitive and do generational dissin' and talk about the music now. I'm not into that, but what I will say is that I've been to places where I've met people who weren't even born in 1996, who said they love Tupac Shakur. I ask why and they say because he taught them not to be scared. He taught me that it's okay to question stuff, it's okay to be vulnerable, it's okay to work hard. People have said to me that Tupac is as big as Bob Marley is in Africa. That is a huge statement. There was a time I went to Barbados years ago, in the early 2000s. Word got around that this brother from America was there, and he was from *Vibe* magazine. People used to call me the Tupac dude, and I respect that. Word got around there in Barbados and a young dude came around with a Tupac T-shirt on, and he said to me, "You don't understand how when I was in jail for seven years, your articles on Tupac saved me and stopped me from dying. I read those articles over and over again, and Tupac's words over and over again." That young man and I just started crying. Fast-forward, in the last ten years I was in an elite private school in Silicon Valley in Northern California. This was a school that was ninety-nine percent white kids, and there was a young white brother sitting in the front row with the Tupac T-shirt on. I asked him who he was. He said, "I'm a student. I'm a president. I'm a quarterback for the football team and I love Tupac." I asked him how he came to love Tupac. He replied: "Because I'm such a big basketball fiend, and my favorite player is Allen Iverson, and so when I fell in love with Allen Iverson, I wanted to know what he listened to, and Allen said he listened to Tupac Shakur, so I became a Tupac Shakur fan." This young man, his father at the time was the CEO of eBay and his mother was the ambassador to the United Nations for President Barack Obama. That is Tupac's impact right there, so many different kinds of people from all over the world.

Tupac created such a wide range of music that it touched a lot of people no matter where they were. The saddest thing is that we never got a chance to see the complete greatness of who he could have been as an actor. We really didn't see the full range of what he could have been as an actor, and yet we still saw a lot. Tupac's impact can be seen with J. Cole, Lupe Fiasco, Kanye West, JAY-Z, Nas, Kendrick Lamar, Lauryn Hill, Cardi B. There's a long list of people who I can hear elements of Tupac in. Definitely Nipsey Hussle. The fact that he got to meet Tupac Shakur's mother and that connection. Nipsey loved Tupac. What I realized over the years is for me not to be sad but understand that Tupac didn't go anywhere. He's still here.

KEVIN POWELL
WRITER
CIVIL AND HUMAN RIGHTS ACTIVIST

LAURA GOVAN

"Tupac was a visionary, and he was everything that these babies aren't today. It is so unfortunate, especially when he was our big brother. Right or wrong, he was our big brother, and when he was wrong, he was still accountable. He would admit that he did something wrong."

I MET TUPAC WHEN I WAS YOUNGER. MY DAD OWNED NIGHTCLUBS throughout Oakland, so we knew all the artists. We knew all the Oakland cats. They all came through in rotation. I remember when Digital Underground came in and we met Tupac. Again, I was young, but I remember seeing this man with an earring in his nose and I just thought to myself, "Who is that?" I remember his gumby fade that was parted, and I thought he was so fine. He always wore a vest, every time he came in. The one thing that stood out the most to me was one day we were at one of my dad's clubs. We were all there, but only to clean. All of a sudden, we heard this commotion. My dad went to look outside and when he opened the door, Tupac was getting into it with these dudes who were trying to fight him. My dad ended up intervening and bringing Tupac inside. Tupac was going off and screaming about this being some bullshit and how the dudes had been trying to fight him for a while. My dad gave him a speech on the wall. My dad told Tupac that he would handle the situation, because throughout Oakland, my dad was highly respected. So, he went outside and when he came back in, he said, "It's good; it's handled," but he told Tupac that he had to get it together. He was willing to give him a chance, but only if he tightened himself up. I guess Tupac listened, because the next time I saw him, he was performing at the club with Digital Underground.

Tupac was always so sweet. I remember anytime I saw him in the club, he would mush me. I thought they were love taps and I always wanted another one. I remember his spirit and him always wanting to do better and be better. He always wanted to get better. He is almost like the living dead. His music still speaks to everybody. Every genre, age group, it doesn't matter. He speaks to them. I feel like he will live forever, even in spirit. It is unfortunate that he is not reachable or touchable. Hip-hop lost a great one. Growing up around such an impactful young man, at such a young age, was amazing, and it saddens me to know that the children of today won't have the same opportunity to know and experience him directly.

I let my children listen to Tupac, or I play a lot of Tupac in my car so that they can get a taste. Lyrically, he is unmatched. The topics he discusses in his music, from politics to real life to the hood to making it and being successful. Everything is in his music. To me, Tupac's music is teaching, like reading an encyclopedia. Situations that he spoke about in his music, such as "Brenda's Got a Baby." Those situations continue to occur, but we seldom speak about it in today's music, and all other music, lyrically, is unmatched. In one of his songs, he speaks about his godson Elijah, and my son's name is Elijah, so the song is relatable to him. The song speaks about him doing better and being better and him being a role model. Tupac lived up to that. Unfortunately, today, hip-hop is not that. It is missing and makes me sad. I had a meeting with Michelle Obama and I expressed how the culture is in music. If you want to connect with the youth, you have to call in the big artist to remake songs such as "We are the world; we are the children." No one does music that way anymore. There isn't any accountability. In today's society, the idea of being a better person for the community is limited. Everyone wants to be a better person for themselves. However, if everyone came together and changed the music industry, which they could because they have the power to, but they don't—everyone is too afraid. That bothers me because everyone says thank you to God, but how do you have faith and have fear? You can't. They do not mix.

Thug Life to me is a couple of things. Thug Life is a grind. A hustle. It isn't about being ghetto. I know a lot of white-collar people who have Thug lives. It means making it. It means hustling. It means getting whatever you desire in whatever way. Whether it be good or bad. Thug Life defines you. Whatever you want that Thug Life to be. It can be sexy. It can be anything, but most importantly, it is a grind.

When I think about how Tupac's vision prepared us for today, I honestly feel as though he would be disappointed. I feel like the vision he set and the platform he put forth is not manifesting today. I do not believe that these kids today get it. I do not believe that the mentors they have in front of them are motivated to help move them. I do not believe that there is any accountability. I believe now it is about All Eyes on Me. Tupac was a visionary, and he was everything that these babies aren't today. It is so unfortunate, especially when he was our big brother. Right or wrong, he was our big brother, and when he was wrong, he was still accountable. He would admit that he did something wrong. I remember when he told the judge that he wasn't perfect. The kids of today don't have that same integrity. They run around telling on one another, and the crazy thing is, they shouldn't even be in that position to tell on somebody and feel as though you have to sell another person out. WE are such a letdown to his vision. Tupac did live the Thug Life, but he did it in a way where he brought others along. He didn't leave anyone behind. Politicians today take heed to the things he said and some of his statements and they use it. No Man Left Behind was something Tupac always talked about. I feel bad for the artists of today because they are missing it. If they did it right, there wouldn't be so many one-hit wonders. I don't feel comfortable playing today's music for my kids. Tupac said things, but he said them politically, respectfully, and with understanding. Half the time, I don't even know what today's artists are even talking about. I feel like today's music is just a headache. I believe that it is the responsibility of the old heads to come together at a round table discussion and take a stand. Talk about how they can bring back the culture of the old music.

With Tupac's music, I could put it on and not press fast-forward. That is what I miss.

LAURA GOVAN
ENTREPRENEUR & PHILANTHROPIST

MACK WILDS

"As scary as it is being a young Black man, it is great to be a Black man."

MY OLDER BROTHERS WERE THE ONES INTRODUCING ME TO HIP-hop. Growing up in Staten Island, we had Wu-Tang, but my oldest brother, Ivory, was from down south, so he was the more eclectic. He introduced me to Outkast, a different type of hip-hop. It was just one time he played Tupac; it was weird—as soon as he started playing Tupac, that's when it played on the radio. It had to be "Brenda's Got a Baby." The things Tupac did, the doors he kicked down. As a New York guy, they tried to downplay his effect on hip-hop, but you can see it everywhere, from how people can do both music and acting. Pac was someone they didn't expect, someone they thought was too gangsta. He was able to show me you can do what you put your mind to. He was the first that allowed me to have the mindset that you can be the product of your environment, but you can be a positive one.

Tupac was fighting for us no matter what. He was the one who allowed others to feel safe to do it. We can have certain rights. Without Pac being able to be that guy, I think there's a lot of us who wouldn't be who we are without him in the back of our minds. When I was in LA, I would throw parties, trying to bring all our friends together. I had just finished with 90210; I got sick on 90210 and it was my first time going out, so I threw a pool party. I remember putting together the footage and thinking what did this day feel like, and I remember playing Tupac's "I Get Around," and I remember it encapsulated that California pool party. It felt like summertime...grilling, pretty girls; he always seemed to encapsulate time in his records. Still to this day, you play it during the summertime, it has this feeling. Just look at hip-hop. You can look at hip-hop and grab your nuts, that "I don't give a fuck" energy he gave. Not saying it started with him, but he exacerbated it. He fans the flame, showing the world, you can be you and not be afraid of what people think, and how coast to coast people walk around with that same energy.

Back in hip-hop during that time, people were specific, if you were conscious or wanted to go the hood route. But Pac was me and I'm not afraid. So you see, that's a lot today, and just how he approached music. You think about Pac recording, how much he was recording, and just his energy. You see it in Wayne, Drake, they live in the recording studio, and I don't know many people besides Prince and Pac. Thug Life to me is a call to every ghetto kid to not be afraid to stand on your own. The one thing I liked about Pac is how he basically said, "They're already going to think and look at us like thugs; it's up to us to decide what that means." Pac made that mean, don't be afraid to be who you are, don't feel like you have to walk in a room and change, feel like you have to abide by any social guidelines, be you. They want you to be a thug or whatever you are, be you. I think he looked at the world for what it could have been. He's one of those guys who wanted more and better for us. He saw the ills of the world. He just wanted more for us. Pac is one of my favorite artists. He inspired me to do poetry; he inspired me to look at the world from different sides and to understand, as scary as it is being a young Black man, it is great to be a Black man.

TRISTAN MACK WILDS
ARTIST

MARSHAWN LYNCH

"Twenty-five years later and you are still relevant to this day. I ain't gonna lie; I'm trying to go out like that. "

I WAS A YOUNGSTER WHEN I WAS FIRST INTRODUCED TO PAC. IT was this big-ass thing; he was really big, but everybody was confused about him. Was Pac from the West Coast or was he from the East Coast? He was from New York, but he lived in Baltimore. He was doing some dancing or whatever. It was so much spiraling around who he really was. It was like, "Oh, Pac is over here in Marin in the Bay Area," and "He fuck with Shock G and Humpty Hump," and, hold on, "He is this close over here?" He really fuck with Spice 1 and he fuck with C-Bo. Pac is fucking-around-in-the-town-type-shit. You start to unpeel, and so I will say that was my first situation. It started to spiral around—and you have to remember at this time, I'm hella young, though. It's all hearsay, creeping in the rooms, listening to either my older brother or some of my older cousins talking about Pac and Digital Underground—I get around. All the niggas in the Bay and Rappin' 4-Tay—they all speak on Pac. This nigga is just dumb-ass intelligent on a whole new level. I started to really get into Tupac; he's on some other shit. Literally, he doesn't give a fuck. That was the first of how I got broke off or introduced to bruh...

For society as a whole from where he was mentally in his mind, as far as the shit that he was speaking and how he would spin it, society wasn't ready for it. In his mind, his vocabulary, everything about him was far more advanced than anybody else. At that time and even to this point, if you just drop Pac right now, a lot of people will not be able to understand where he was coming from. That is just me and my opinion based on how I feel. It's more so how I see people pick and choose to take certain advice, certain people read the Bible, and they only apply certain shit to their life that's good for them at that time, or for what they want to come out of it. And not overall, the whole shit, I say that because we live in a foul-ass world

201

right now, and at that time, if you listen to Pac, on his Pac shit, on his hit 'em up shit, Nigga, I'm about to go, I don't give a fuck, whatever it take, nigga, that's how I'm coming, but in reality, that's what he had toward an individual. Now you see that everybody takes that type of flame and puts that shit out for the world, into the world. Individuals will take what they feel is for them, and apply it to how they believe it.

From his acting, it was no doubt to the world that he was a talented individual. Seeing him in movies, even the hardest nigga outside right now are like, "Man, if I got the chance to act in a movie, I would go in that mutherfucker and act like Pac." Pac has always been Pac in his roles, and he does his thing the way he does it. He went into that Hollywood role, with acting in it, and was himself. The way he speaks on activism or the way that I interpret and the way I listen to him speak about injustice. He made people understand that you're not about to talk over my head. I can speak your language; I can come to you on any level you want, whether it is the top of the top, to a CEO, or the politician. Or, you the janitor at the building I just walked into and signed my multi-million-dollar deal. To the hardest gangster on the street to the pimp, the crackheads and to the wino, he was so well spoken. He put it out there for every individual to let you know that he felt your pain and that he was speaking to you and your position. Not you in somebody else's position but you in your position.

I think people pick and choose how they want to receive it and choose to make the changes that they want to make. The heart of change is two different approaches; we're either going to live in unison or we're going to rise up and we live on our own. Now it's going to take a strong mindset and change for it to happen. Those were the seeds that he was planting while he was here on Earth. A lot of people still understand it, but overall, society always wins. As long as you put an individual in front of the camera and get a Black face. If you get a Black face in there, you keep the majority of our niggas in the same place that they're in. I feel he did us justice and injustice at the same time. From the acting, activism, and music, I don't believe you can put nobody lyrically just from being diverse. This nigga go make a party song and then makes a song about why we need to stand up and rise against police brutality. "Dear Mama" to "Brenda's Got a Baby." In that situation alone, I look at this situation with my own eyes. I know so many Brendas' right now that got a baby. Were y'all listening to the same song that I was listening to? Like damn, little Mama, he told you to keep your p**** in your pants and you will be alright. For everything that he was saying, it was always something for everybody.

If you would have asked me about Thug Life five, ten years ago, I would have a different answer for you. Now, at thirty-five, Thug Life to me is protecting and taking care of my family by any means necessary. If it comes to all that shit that portrays me as a thug and that's what's about to get done because I want to last, not come in last. If it comes to that, quote, unquote thug head bussing—and all the other things, then that's what it comes to. Realistically, that shit is about gang-style-gangster shit, protecting my family, making sure we all are able to eat, we don't have to worry about shit, we are about living our lives, in the manner in which we choose.

When it comes to change, I am going to say the way it didn't change. We are still doing the same shit we were doing back when MLK was marching; now fast-forward to 2020. You have people marching for George Floyd. As far as history repeating itself, I believe him being here right now, would mean much more to be that dominant voice and echoing that change is going to have to come from us instead of it being led by organizations which have been coming out of nowhere. When you're talking about the Black faces who are standing in front and you know that the Black face would have been a real one. One that was really meant for what we have going on. In terms of listening to his music and actually seeing the shit that he talked about in the early '90s is coming to fruition. To this day you can go and listen to whoever is whoever and they will tell you that Pac was this and Pac was that. They will sample something Pac had going on. This is how he affected our culture. That monkey or that devil, that mutherfucker is strong in keeping us where we are; it is really strong. I think about how he has sculpted me. I ain't gonna lie; if I get into a position, depending on what type of situation it is, whether they're talking, "Marshawn did not stand up for the anthem" or something like that. Now, I go and listen to some of his music, depending on my mood, thinking that maybe I am on the right path; maybe I am thinking the right way. The way that I move is really silent, and it is more about the action that I really do. I don't want to compare myself to him as far as the things that are going on. That is where I would draw the line and be different. I will go out and make that shit happen. I will do whatever it is that I am thinking, rather than going on somebody's platform or TV show. I'm not a damn rapper, so I'm not going to put it in a damn song. I'm just going to go and do that type of shit that I'm thinking. Even to the point where I go out and do my little acting shit. Which is hard. I'm going to go and try that shit. I watch Pac do it, hell yeah, I wanna do that shit. I sat and talked to one of my cousins. We say to each other, Ay, man, we need to go 'head and make a remake of *Juice*. We should go ahead and remake the motherfucking *Above the Rim* n' shit. We can do a skit and remake that; everybody wanted to go play that motherfucking Pac role.

It goes two ways; it's really important to me because at the end of the day, I don't want to see any of my family not being able to eat. At the same time, that old-ass saying, "You give a person a fish, they eat for one day; if you teach them how to fish, fam can feed himself for the rest of his life." That's more the path I feel I take when I do what I do for my family. Whatever somebody else has going on, big ups to them. If they're not in my family and in my circumference, my arms reach more power to you. I respect what you're doing, but it has nothing to do with me. Keep doing what you are doing if it is working for you.

I was ten and look at the effects it has on me, twenty-five years later. That's how you know that nigga was strong; I was ten. For all those years I've been singing those goddamn songs, I didn't have a motherfucking clue what I was talking about. I'm ten, so I was for sure doing all the Humpty Hump dances thinking, "When I get older, I will have a pool party just like that; I will be running around chasing girls with little-bitty drawers on." I will have all my cousins, my brothers with me. Doing the Humpty Dance, we were talking about I get around, no shirt on, with my gold chain running around, with my super-soaker wetting them up like, "Come here, girl."

I had no idea what I was talking about, talking about "I get around." I get around to what? "Get around" to doing your homework, boy, with yo dumb ass. You can't even read and you talk about you "get around." You don't get around shit. Here, read this book, and then I will tell you if you will get around. You will get around to some ADD courses and some goddamn Ritalin if you don't go and sit your hot ass down. Boy, what's wrong with you? Even being ten years old, listening to his music and doing a reference to his music. Now, in my thirties, when they're talking about "Marshawn is a criminal," "Marshawn is a thug," or "He just one of those ghetto-ass niggas from

Oakland." Not any of these recent rappers, I'm going to listen to a rapper who I listened to when I was ten years old. It's not that I'm going to get clarity and understanding, but you were going through the same shit that I was going through. You were on the outside and a bit more militant than the kid, but nigga, the same shit that you were talking about then, I can say the same shit. They're coming at me from all different types of angles when all I'm trying to do is put on for my people. I'm trying to educate my people and y'all making me a menace to society. How the fuck is that even possible? That's how that shit works, huh? Twenty-five years later, and you are still relevant to this day. I ain't gonna lie; I'm trying to go out like that.

When you are hollering at the next retired NFL player, whoever it is, "What do you think about Marshawn? How do you think that nigga made a contribution?" I don't know, man, don't nobody really know about that nigga, man. I don't know. I see that nigga everywhere, but I never knew what the fuck he had. It's gone happen; I got a lot of shit to do...I appreciate you letting me be a part of this. I would've loved to meet him. Well, now I'm in the position I'm in, I've met a couple of people that've been around him. Everybody wants to claim Pac, wherever Pac went. Pac from the town, Pac was over in the jungles in Marin. He was getting down over there; that shit is really mind-blowing. I will tell you straight up, I have been a part of some shit and did not go and be part of some shit, that I probably know that maybe I should have turned down. I turned down going to the White House when we had a Black president. This is one thing that I could not turn down; I had to be a part of this, so thank you, sis.

MARSHAWN LYNCH "BEASTMODE"
DADDI

206

MIKE G

"You could feel his energy. From his performance to his songs, you could only wish to have that type of fan love, as an artist. You could only wish to be able to express that emotion, no matter what it is. Whether positive or negative, you could feel his emotion in songs."

MY FIRST INTRODUCTION TO PAC WAS HIM WITH DIGITAL Underground. We were in Cali around the same time they dropped the Humpty Hump. I didn't see him, but I heard about him. Everybody was saying he was from New York. Although we never had any real run-ins, I heard he used to run with somebody from 113th Street. His name always came up in circles. When he dropped "Brenda's Got a Baby," I really dug it. It was more conscious than what the Humpty Hump and Digital Underground were. It was obvious that he was going in a different direction, and I respected that. There wasn't much conscious rap. The way he told the story was great. I always appreciate a good storyteller. That is my strength and I was happy. There are some songs you hear that are just all right. When you heard Tupac, it was a solid song, and that's what I enjoyed.

He had a great work ethic. During his early years, he was zipping around a lot. It's easier when you are solo than when you are in a group. There is nothing wrong with being in a group; you have to go through more moving parts. Everybody has to be in sync before you can make a move. He was like Ping, Pong, Ping Pong, Ping.

As the saying goes, "You're known best for your last record," or "the thing you did last." With Pac, there was "Brenda's Got a Baby," which is how I measured it, through the songs. That's your biggest voice. When you're speaking to people, "Brenda's Got a Baby," "Dear Mama," all of the allegations, the whole Suge Knight stuff, the way he keyed into that demographic. I'm just over fifty, he is turning fifty, the way his energy really spearheaded our generation, playing the fine line, and being responsible, not just for himself. Being responsible for his people, his family, and the street culture. It's hard to call it activism. His role and his identity were important and were needed. He was a firecracker, and that energy has been unmatched. You don't find that type of energy and the type of love from the public to an artist. Also through ups and downs, people have always stayed with him. He wore his feelings on his sleeve.

He will speak about it. Which is cool, because that's what you want at the end of the day. You want some type of truth. I have strayed a bit from activism. I didn't see him like that. I saw and felt his energy, which was important, and he was definitely a voice.

A lot of artists see his work ethic and try to match his energy. Depending on the type of artist you were. I haven't seen that type of work ethic from an artist up until then. I would categorize myself in the older school of artists. Biz was one of those that really went hard. People didn't see it, but he went hard as far as recording, putting out songs, just his overall work ethic. There are a couple of others. Biz was the first one to come to mind. People trying to copycat Thug Life. Pac is almost like James Brown, whereas you could make a catalog of the songs he is referenced in. Maybe not the beat sample, but there are so many songs that he is referenced in. It could be a game show question. That's his biggest asset, or was his biggest asset, his work ethic. He was rolling and doing his thing. I've got mixtapes where I heard some of the *Makaveli* songs before they came out on that one album.

This is not my favorite Tupac story, but it is a Tupac story. The Source Awards, in '90, '92. 'Tip went on and he and Tupac's shows overlapped. This made it appear as Pac was cutting him off. And boy! Cats were hot! Everybody was hot, hot, hot! These were the pre-Suge days.

So that happened, and it was nearing the end of the show. Afterward, everybody was going to a club that was on Fourteenth Street. The street was blocked off and everybody was in the street. It was me, 'Tip, and I believe Maseo, along with somebody else, and

Pac was there. He could have been with another person. Everybody walks up to him like, "Yo, what's up with that?" I was on the side. You could see on his face that it was an honest mistake. He explained that they told him to go on and he went. He was sincere about it. That is one thing I saw in him. Even when he jumped on stage, you could see his kind of newness. That new-school shine, it was a big deal to be at the Source Awards.

That was my first meeting with him and he was cool. You could feel his energy. From his performance to his songs, you could only wish to have that type of fan love, as an artist. You could only wish to be able to express that emotion, no matter what it is. Whether positive or negative, you could feel his emotion in songs. I remember that about him the most. I don't think any other artist has or could compare to that, not that I've seen. There's a lot of people trying in the industry now, right after Pac. Many clones have come out, and you're never going to get that type of emotion, that true emotion. Through hip-hop in our culture, in that form, when his moon comes around, he is going to spit out a little baby. Somebody's really going to be reminiscent of Pac; it hasn't come around yet.

It's fast food right now, and they're taking advantage of it. There's a lot of good music out here, but it is so few and far between. It's really hard to distinguish what's authentic and what's factory-made. We are fortunate to have come up in the time of Pac. Fortunately, he was able to swing and carry that vibe. Being from New York and really growing on the West Coast, he still had that vibe. He could capture the east as well as the west; even though he was all West Coast love, there was a time when people from New York were like, fuck Pac. He still had a lot of love out here and he still has a lot of love.

Thug Life is doing what you have to do to get by, by any means necessary, to a certain extent.

The police and his incident in Atlanta were definitely a trailer to what we have happening now. Going back to "Brenda's Got a Baby," his whole first album, the things he was saying then are really still what's happening now. He was grown-man status even back then.

Salute to Pac, his work ethic, and his energy. I look forward to seeing when his moon passes and he drops his jewels on somebody else. It doesn't seem like twenty-five years have passed; that's hard to swallow, but it's solid, too. That shows his legacy is intact and you can speak of him like he passed five years ago.

MIKE G
JUNGLE BROTHER

MONEY B

"A lot of times we as people want to claim ownership of someone, but you can't claim ownership of Tupac. There are going to be movies and books about Tupac until the end of time because he impacted so many, and there are so many amazing stories."

THE FIRST TIME I MET TUPAC WAS ON THE CORNER OF THIRTY-Ninth and Market at the border of West Oakland and North Oakland. It was outside of a house that Shock G and Sleuth, my manager at the time, were living in. I was called there because Atron Gregory was considering signing this new group called Strictly Dope and he wanted them to audition for us. What I understand is that Tupac had already auditioned for Shock separately, but this was the first time we were meeting the entire group. These three dudes jumped out of the car and they stood on the corner and they started rapping. I was listening and I thought they were all right. I always tell people that I thought that Ray Luv and Tupac were equally talented as rappers. When they rhymed, because they had routines, they were rhyming off of each other. I thought okay, this is cool. Tupac had this energy, this charisma about him. When you were in a room with him, the attention went toward him. He had something good to say about everything. He was playing in the room because he was trying to get on. He was savvy like that, even from the very beginning. He knew how to work it. That was the introduction.

Tupac and I became close because we were close in age; Ray was a little younger. Where I lived at the time, my block was active, and inside my apartment it was active. My apartment was hip-hop. He was attracted to be around this real grimy environment that had all hip-hop inside it. Whenever they came to Oakland to record, he would always come by my place. I had the turntables, females, dudes outside selling dope. He liked being around, and he would always stop by. That is how the relationship developed. Yes, my father was in the Black Panther Party, but that wasn't what connected us. The way that correlated was when he would speak about certain things, the message I was already familiar with because I grew up the same way. When he talked about things, he didn't have to explain it twice to me. I knew what he was talking about and I was cool with it. Whereas other people looked at him like he was crazy and he had to explain it or educate people, and he didn't have to do that with me. In that aspect, that is how that worked. We didn't have to spend our time talking about those things, and in turn we focused our minds on working and figuring out how we were going to get this demo together. We were both working on demos at the same time even though I was in Digital Underground. They were working on Strictly Dope at the time before they broke up. We were just trying to get it. That's how the bond really started. He knew that he could come around me and he could be himself and he could talk about it, and I could ask him and talk about it and we understood each other. When I tell people that, they still look at me like they don't understand and that is okay. I don't mind. Now, as an adult, I still ask the elders about certain things because I understand things differently. As a child I didn't ask much about the Black Panther Party, but all I knew was the Black Panther Party.

Tupac's music still affects society because the message is, as much as technology has advanced and other things have changed, socially we haven't changed much. We like to claim that we're different, but we still are the same. I remember Tupac talking about equality. We're not trying to be better; we just want to be treated fairly. Now, Tupac would always say that we should take equality. He had this warrior mentality of going out and getting what you wanted. A lot of the issues we saw then are still present today. That is why it is very relevant and that is why his music and his message and his words will always be relevant. I don't know if in our lifetime things will change that much.

Tupac's activism is seen in his first album *2Pacalypse Now*. I remember him making it and I remember being proud of the music he was making. I was proud because when I did my music, I would probably put one or two songs with such a message, but with Tupac, he would put his full heart into it. His full album would be filled with these messages scattered throughout the entire album. I loved it. We would always joke with each other because he was always this warrior who was ready to go to war. All in all, I was happy for the music he was making at the time. So much so that I remember the first time I heard *All Eyez on Me*. The last time I saw Pac, I was in the House of Blues that summer of '96 and it was shortly after the album came out. I saw him and I told him I didn't know because that album sounded as though it was vengeful and spiteful and it was a message that I hadn't heard in the previous albums. It wasn't a balance like it usually was, and I told him that. He said, "Oh, nah, I'm going to get back to it, but I just have to get this stuff off my chest." I said, okay, I don't know if I like that. That album just didn't feel like the messages I heard before, and I expressed that to him and he didn't take it any kind of way. He understood, and him saying that he just had to express himself and get this stuff off his chest, I understood.

One of the memories I have of Pac truly showed how charismatic he was. I was noticing it and it wasn't until we did the video for "Doowutchyalike." The video wasn't out, but we were performing in the Bay Area and the song was released around there and Digital Underground had "Underwater Rimes," which was out and it was being recognized. So locally we had it poppin'. We were shooting the "Doowutchyalike" video and I was telling people Tupac was around back then, but he was in another group but he was still around us. So our video was about to come out and this was maybe a year after high school. There was this one girl that liked me in high school who came home from college. I invited her to come over because we were editing the video. She came over and this girl was in love with me. I could do no wrong. She came over and Tupac was over there as well and we were joking and laughing. I just happened to look over at her and she was following every movement of Tupac's lips and she was just looking at him as he was talking. I'm looking at her and I'm looking at him and I'm looking at her and I go, okay, I get it! I didn't say anything to him but I was like, okay, this might be right. This might be it. That was the first time I realized that yep, he's got to be a star.

The funny thing is, I don't even really know what Thug Life is about or what it means. I do know that whatever he thought it meant or said, I was with it. So if today it meant that we were going to get our guns and shoot these niggas, then that's what we were going to do. If the next day it meant that we were going to give out hugs and flowers, then I was with it. Whatever he felt that it was like, I was with it.

Tupac had a lot of ideas of where he thought we could go, but we haven't been there yet. Pac wanted to open restaurants. He wanted to do a clothing line and he wanted to educate the youth. He had so many ideas in his mind and he didn't understand why we couldn't achieve them. Everyone thought he was crazy, but you fast-forward and it's clear that it all could be done. Nipsey was the evolution to what Tupac planned. If it wasn't for Tupac, we wouldn't have believed that we could do these things that we're doing now. Nipsey came from dirt and just carried it and raised the bar. Somebody's going to come along and draw from what Nipsey did and take it even further. However, it all started from Tupac believing that we could and really stressing that we could and that he could and really going for it. I'll look around and everybody wants to start a clothing line. Everybody wants to do this and do that. We didn't really do these things. We might have thought that we could or we wanted to, but we didn't, or we weren't progressively reaching for our goals the way that Tupac told us that we could. We saw him do so much at the age of twenty-five. Any twenty-five-year-old could look at Tupac and think, what am I doing with my life? Tupac made us believe that we could do anything.

When we first started out, only because I was on a tour with a record that I had a little bit of notoriety and because I was older, that I was the big bro. I was giving him direction on what he should do when he went on tour and went on the road. At the end of it, he became the big brother because I began looking at him and understood that no one had the work ethic that he had and the drive and the determination to do what he wanted to do. I draw from that as if he is the big bro. Now when I am doing something, I know what hard work looks like, so I can't say that I'm working hard and I'm not working as hard as I could. That's what I mean when I say draw from that. Since I know what it looks like, you can't approach me with any bullshit. You can't tell me that you want to be an artist and I tell you to do this and that and you give me excuses. I have a checklist, and in my head, if you're not doing these things, then you're not trying to achieve your goals. You can't question me about that because I saw what a real work ethic is through Tupac.

I was looking at a picture recently of me, Tupac, and Shock. I think it was from Summer Jam 92, and I'm the only person that can tell that story or the story behind that picture. What is so amazing is that Tupac touched so many people. I run into people and they tell me these great stories and I am amazed. A lot of times we as people want to claim ownership of someone, but you can't claim ownership of Tupac. He touched so many people. When the movie *All Eyez on Me* came out, so many people had something to say. However, there are going to be movies and books about Tupac until the end of time, because he impacted so many, and there are so many amazing stories. I have my own stories, but I am sure others have their own amazing stories. None of us hold all the pieces to the puzzle. All of us hold a piece to the puzzle, which is theirs. I won't devalue anybody's piece or raise mine above anybody else. I am just glad that he was able to touch so many. I am looking forward to hearing as many of these stories that I possibly can, from as many people that I am fortunate enough to meet who will share with me. If someone else does another book or another movie, I am going to support that as well, because I think that as much as we can learn and know, we should.

MONEY B
DIGITAL UNDERGROUND

OMARI HARDWICK

"I felt lonely before Pac; I felt so misunderstood, but Pac understood me."

I WOULD SAY I WOULD HAVE TO THANK SHOCK G (RIP). I WAS listening to the radio with Shock G doing a loose introduction to the roadie Tupac. You hear Pac in the background, I just remembered his voice, then one way or another, my ears landed on the "Same Song." Then I did my research and remember, there was no Alexa or Google, but I figured out New York, activist, Afeni, then Baltimore, Jada...So I started to learn about his aptitude for theatre, his sensitivity. I just heard things in my household. Then I stayed connected to him through college, and staying attached that I even introduced his music to my moms, the first MC I ever did that for, and she felt it. You know what it was, I felt lonely before Pac; I felt so misunderstood, but Pac understood me. I just really aligned with Tupac, and it made sense why he and Biggie weren't really in alignment, because they have the same Zodiac sign. I feel like it's pervasive there every day. I don't know if we were fighting a wrongful death and the hand of white cops holding Black guns, shooting Black kids, different conversation, Black hand, holding a Black gun, shooting fellow Black kid/man. You and I are now the ones to let white folks go, "What about that?" No, no, we talk about that every day.

Pac is so influential; it didn't start with George Floyd crying for his mom but with Pac's cry for Afeni. I think he's as influential as I am when the monikers called and went against the grain. I remember thinking LL COOL J went against the grain by making a love song "I Need Love." I remember thinking Chuck D and Flavor Flav were doing something different. I definitely remember thinking cats on the West Coast were on to something, calling out cops. I remember thinking these things but remembering Pac was so good and Gemini out, meaning his wingspan was bigger than Scottie Pippen's times thirty that he was able to take all of those going-against-the-grain moments and put them in his heart, but also in his music.

Pac would never have had an issue with Em; he would have been proud of his pen, proud that he honored him, but he would have said, you shouldn't talk about putting your mom in the trunk. But Pac was so influential, that I don't know if there's a person who influenced our biggest Anglo-Saxon MC, who goes down as one of the top ten ever, outside of Pac. He's the most influential for Eminem; he's the most influential for when George Floyd was crying out on the pavement. As a big human and dying on the floor for eight minutes and whatever seconds. I think Pac...I don't know if our beautiful brother Tyson Beckford, and Beth Anne, who reminds me of you, got a lot of your power. I don't really know if Kadeem's mama aids Polo Brown the way she was able to while fighting Tyson Beckford in a park, in some part of New York. I don't really know if it goes that route if Pac wasn't Pac. I think he is so beyond icons like James Dean, people that died young, Jimi Hendrix, they are so beyond art that the activism in their art just becomes a way of life. They are just a way of life. I always tell Nova, my eight-year-old daughter, "Where the wind blows, Nova, that's God carrying your dreams." Pac to me, Aiyisha, is like that wind. He affects everyone who walks outside, and inside, because he's rebellious enough for the right reasons. He was misunderstood for the wrong reason. He imparted grace and mercy on everyone. I believe that when he died, in the quiet of the quiet, he was able to eradicate that which he asked his cousin to do in terms of the visual you painted for me saying, "Hey, Biggie, he doesn't want to see you." I believe he is so powerful and in his quietness, he was able to go, "I love Biggie." Pac is a monument.

Thug Life means the hate you give...as Pac said. It doesn't necessarily mean what Malcolm said early on. Tupac didn't believe this meant, okay, I'm going to go out and get crazy. The way I'm talking to Tupac's cousin is the way he would talk to Tabitha Sorenson from MTV. He loved Tabitha. I was so into Pac I would watch anything that he did. But they would have these great interviews. Pac wasn't like Malcolm in hurting a faction of people but was going to talk about the hate that was given to us. I'm going to rock out in a way that brings it to the attention of those who are ignoring the fact of what's going down. It was my junior year at the University of Georgia in the Peach Bowl playing the University of Virginia. We went out to this club, The Warehouse, and I had seen your cousin, as I stated, and saw him get on stage and rock and know how much I cared about him without ever meeting him. He walked past us in the club, and in particular me at five ten, and Pac's what, five nine. So we looked at each other but it made me think, I got to see this dude again, 'cause that was my moment and it didn't work, but I'm about an organic moment. So when I met him, it was at the speakeasy, and it was spoken-word night and Pac was in the corner taking in poetry, and he had a bag clutched under his arm, and these cool spectacles. I didn't know he wore glasses and all his things. He was smooth, I walked over to him, shot my shot, and said I saw you a couple of years back perform, and I said if I could, I'd find the moment to tell you how much you meant to me. I reached out in shock and he went, "I really do appreciate you," and that was the first and last time. His juggle has prepared us for the diversified world we live in. He prepared us on how to focus on what is the priority. Pac was such a hands-on guy. But Pac absolutely was a juggler of sorts, he went to the studio and never left. Pac has set us in motion for the motion. That's why it was shocking when I met him, because he was still, and I didn't know him to be that. I wasn't presented with him being that way. That's why I think Tabitha and him were cool, because I think he felt those white people really rocked out for him and they felt he was misunderstood. He allows us to keep up with these technological advances. We got to remember there was no real big Steve Jobs movie being made but Pac was righteously ready. Pac is a monument.

OMARI HARDWICK
ACTOR, PRODUCER, POET, ARTIST

PORTIA KIRKLAND

"Tupac was a prophet who ministered
in his own way with a calling on his life."

M Y AUNT ELAINE WAS A FORMER PANTHER AND A FRIEND OF Geronimo "G" Pratt, Tupac's godfather. One day my aunt told me that Tupac and I had a lot in common. We were both passionate about our people, loved God and hip-hop, had roots in the movement, and we were both in the music industry. This mix of being in the entertainment industry and in the movement is often a challenge because what God calls you to is often in direct conflict with what the entertainment world requires of you to become a star. So, I think what's dope about Tupac is he was true to himself, and didn't compromise his calling. He had a global impact on the world and touched people not just by being a dope rapper, but by ministering hope. Yes, Tupac was an incredible artist and actor, but clearly, he was a man of purpose. If you follow Tupac's career, you'll see how he eloquently demonstrated that you have to meet people where they are. You can't minister to the streets unless you've been in them. You can't lead the sheep without a testimony. You can't minister to the poor with such a deep purpose unless you've gone hungry. You can't encourage children of addicts and offer hope unless you've been there. Tupac was a legend, and I think God blessed him with enormous talent, whether rapping or acting, not just to win awards and sell records, but to encourage people and change the world. This is why Tupac would have a record about the streets, and then on the next song tell people to keep their head up. He knew he was called for more than just entertaining people. And this is what sets Tupac apart from the rest—he had the courage and audacity to answer his calling.

Something unique that I remember about Tupac was his work ethic. He took writing seriously. While the entertainment industry can be a lot of fun, there was always this sense of "We can't play too long; I have to get this out." That's what happens when you have a ministry, a calling on your life, and you have to get it out because you know it's not for you; it's for the people. A seed is planted and when it's time to give birth, it's time. He knew he had a calling on his life. As painful as it was to lose Tupac, like Malcolm and MLK, he was flawed, but he also was chosen by God. When we reflect back to many of Tupac's interviews, it was a bit too deep for people to catch the first time because women were in love with his looks and men connected with his struggle. But now, as you reflect back, you see that Tupac was dropping jewels, but they went over people's heads at the time. Now, his words of wisdom are being studied worldwide.

Infamous court scene

I remember the day when we were all at court and Tupac was surrounded by close friends and family. His heart was heavy. He was frustrated and felt that he was being unfairly convicted. He was being targeted, and the man that gave hope to so many, was losing hope himself. We all tried to encourage Tupac. Before exiting court, we managed to calm Tupac down. His voice softened and we all discussed the next steps for Tupac's court case. As we exited and Tupac saw the media, I think something struck a chord in him that said he had already lost the case before it started, not because he was guilty but because of a broken system not built to protect him. Tupac began spitting at the cameras, and no matter how much we attempted to utter words of encouragement and ease, Tupac felt defeated and acted out in anger. I think this is typical of any Black man who is told over and over again you don't have a chance when you know it's your right to plead your case in a court of justice. I'll never forget that day because this was Tupac saying "F the system," and his refusal to accept the assassination of his character. He felt betrayed because Tupac was fully committed to his people and his community.

PORTIA KIRKLAND
COMMUNICATIONS AND MARKETING EXECUTIVE

PRINCESS MDAIYAH EFUA-ATA YISRAEL

"I think that his message and how he died still affects our generation today."

I THINK THAT HIS MESSAGE AND HOW HE DIED STILL AFFECTS OUR generation today. Even the younger generation, like my children, have questions and wonder what the outcome was. And then you can see, I don't recall the rapper's name who kinda redid a remake of his song...I can't think of his name, I'd probably have to ask the children, but they play it all the time. And they'll play that, and then they'll play Pac's version and it just shows me how they're still connected and how he's still connected to the world. Some of these children weren't even born when he passed. 'Cause I was in my first year of college, so I know my children weren't born. And even the rapper I think that did the song, he wasn't born. When I first heard it, I was like, "Woah!" Then they played his song and I noticed that that's what they do. He's still a part of everybody's life.

The memory that I guess stands out the most is when we were coming from court, I believe, and reporters were coming around. And I can't remember if the reporters were coming toward me and he told them to get away or if it was vice versa. But it was after the case when the police officer got shot in Atlanta. I can't remember if we were coming into the courthouse or leaving. But they were bombarding us with cameras, and I believe that's when he came and was like, "Yo, get out her face," and just protecting and saying what he said. You know, that Tupac riled-up energy. But that's probably my lasting memory because I was older. And after that, I don't think I had too many visits with him after that, besides at the family house. A couple years later, he passed.

Another memory I have is from a Tupac concert at The Warehouse. Gosh, how old were we? He was performing and it was all of us in there, family everywhere. And so, we were all dancing, me and my sisters and cousins. And then one of the guys from H-Town started hitting on one of my sisters. And instead of him just taking "no" for an answer, he thought we were just, I guess, fans of Tupac or whatever, just some club hoppers. He basically got a little violent, called her a "b," I believe at that time, either myself or one of my sisters went and found our brothers, because they were in the club. And before you know it, we had them surrounded. One of my brothers, I think, went and broke a bottle, I think it was Ish, and had it in his hand. Like, they didn't even see us. And I just remember Chaka coming, basically before it got too out of hand, and was like, "Yo, that's Pac's family! Blah, blah, blah...Y'all 'bout to start a war up in here!" And some girl he was with tried to step to us or whatever. But basically, at the end of it, he had to come and try to apologize, and he was just like, "Yo, I ain't know y'all was so deep." 'Cause once it settled down, everybody came and it was a crowd of us there.

Oh yeah: "Y'all better go. 'Cause it's about to..." So they dispersed. And I guess that's just how it was, 'cause every club we went to...

To me, it's just who we are. For me, I raised my children with the concept that we're strong. I have strong Black sons; I have strong Black daughters. And that there's nowhere in this life that you can go where you don't use your voice, you don't stand up and be strong. And there's nobody who's over you besides the Creator. So when I think about it, you know people kinda take "thug" as, you gotta be ruthless and carry guns. But I tell my children, it's all about who you are inside, it's the intellect that you have, and because we know what Thug Life stood for, how we were trained, it's kind of like a matter of fact that we teach our children now. So for me, it's just about who we are. And we're not thugs on the streets, but we, you know...

In that era, when he was out, you had a lot of different mixtures of music, so what he represented because of who he was and who we are to him, it just made me feel like our voices were being heard more than anything.

236

I think society was influenced more with just being able to relate to someone. Because he didn't come from a rich family. So I think they were able to relate because he was just a real person. He just spoke the truth. It was who he was. During that time, I know the male classmates in my school just felt like somebody was able to hear them. So that's how he influenced society with his music. His activism, I think for us—like children of the movement—it just showed us that we have different formats on how we can be active, and we don't have to repeat what our parents did, we can actually put the message out there and do the work in a different format that is fit for who we are and not necessarily who they are. I just felt like people saw a different side of who we are through him. Like, we're not victims; we're not poor, sad children. We have a voice and we're able to vocalize what we lived through.

PRINCESS MDAIYAH EFUA-ATA YISRAEL
ADMINISTRATOR
DOULA
GARDENER
SHEPHERDESS

RALPH
MCDANIELS

"His music touched the people in the street. Regular folk. Sometimes artists just make party music and Tupac gave us a balance. He talked about topics in his songs that touched people."

I WAS FIRST INTRODUCED TO TUPAC THROUGH MY VIDEO SHOW, Video Music Box. He was featured on a Digital Underground song. When I saw him I inquired about who he was. He didn't look like or sound like the rest of the group. I heard him when I was in Oakland, I was working on a project for Toni Tony! Tone! and I heard the song on a mixtape. I said Oh okay and then I saw the video and I was like Ok. I hadn't been paying too much mind to the fact that he was there all that time. I didn't see that.

When it came to the influence his music had on me, I was glad that there was an artist who was representing back nationalism in the music industry and in hip hop. I felt that's what he was doing in his music. I was happy to see that. I am a product of hip hop so we looked for artists like that in Pubic Enemy and X-Clan. So I felt he was in that same vein.

His music touched the people in the street. Regular folk. Sometimes artists just make party music, but Tupac gave us a balance. He talked about topics in his songs that touched people.

Especially his first couple of albums. I felt his music was so important for the community because like I said, my parents came up in the sixties with Malcom X, Martin Luther King and Huey Newton. I am all of that but I am also in the entertainment business, so I listened to consciousness and I thought it was dope. Tupac was able to balance that out and make it palpable for those who could get it. I also worked with Pac on Juice and I watched him come to NY and he was the only person that the production company hired. The production team brought me on because they really could not get the Hip Hop Community to grab on to what they were doing. We didn't know Pac at the time and when they said we got Tupac, we were like, who is Tupac? They brought me in, they introduced me to Tupac and I realized that this was the guy from Digital Underground. I hung out with him and took him around and he did know a few people because he was on tour with Digital Underground and had in NY. We went to different places. I watched him as a regular dude. Tupac had the ability to come into a town and automatically attract everything that was popping. It started with the women. All of sudden there are all these women and I am asking myself, where did all these women come from. They all would come to set especially after he started to tell everyone he was going to be in a movie. I saw it grow from 5 people to 500 hundred people.

Our relationship was I'm the OG/Uncle and he was the nephew. Anytime we would see each other, we would check if the other was good and that was that. He always wanted to connect with the like minds in the community. He wanted to get with the creative heads. He wanted to connect with those that thought like him and that was what he did. We connected in the day and partied in the night.

Tupac had a universal appeal or energy that most people did not have. He had a free spirit and spoke his mind. A lot of people did not have or were afraid to speak their mind like he did so they looked at him and were in awe, because he said what they wanted to say. Tupac being in the entertainment business, he had a higher platform to attract people. Everything he was saying was going on would really happen. That attracted a lot of people. He connected to me because of my platform and our relationship took off from there. He was who he said he was. Especially in his early career. He was the real deal.

THUG Life was about understanding that sometimes you have to thug it out with whatever situation you are in. America is a THUG. So, if you are not about that THUG life then it is going to be difficult for you to be somebody or achieve something. You have to be about that THUG life.

I think that Tupac wanted people to be self-sufficient and not depend on anybody. He believed in having your own. Have your own, not working for anybody. Even if it was going somewhere, you could do it and do it freely. As a black man in NY at the time it was simply hard to catch a cab. His vision was focused on changing that kind of world.

When he was working on the set of Juice, he was the first character casted. At the same time, Diddy wanted to be in Juice. I remember Diddy calling me inquiring about the role of Bishop, but Tupac was already locked in.When he was on set, he would get into arguments with Omar Epps and the other actors because he felt that they weren't taking the opportunity as seriously as he was. He would tell them, I came all the way from California and I am going to make sure this changes my life. Y'all are not taking it seriously. Stop fucking around and let's get into this." After that, everyone was on point. He brought another level of professionalism and passion to set. He would always give 120 percent. Witnessing Pac bring that character to life was memorable. Growing up there were always brothers who were thugs or a little bit on the edge that you did not want to deal with at all. Yet, you saw how that person still had potential to do other things. In the film, he gave hope to those kinds of people who couldn't quite tell you how they were feeling. but they knew what they wanted. Bishop was that person though it didn't end the way it was supposed to end.

If someone else was casted in the role then I don't believe that Bishop would have been as charismatic. That was the appeal and that is why it is a classic film, a hip hop classic.

RALPH MCDANIELS
VIDEO MUSIC BOX
TEACHER

RAY LUV

"I said I don't think I'm allowed in Marin City; that sounds dangerous for me. He said, 'No, don't worry about it. If they get you, they gotta get both of us.' That was the first day I met him. That was the beginning of our friendship."

M Y STORY STARTS WITH PAC BEFORE WE EVER MET. AT THAT time, around 1988, there weren't that many rap groups in my area. There was just a handful. Me and Mac Dre, this was even before we heard of E-40. Pac had a group called One Nation MCs of Marin City, and that was a time before four-track tapes. Me and DJ Dize, who became the DJ for Pac and me later on, we would make four-track tapes. They would be passed around through the girls and through the homies, so I was familiar with his voice and his lyrics to a certain extent, but I knew him as part of a conglomerate. One day Leila Steinberg, who was my first manager and one of Pac's first managers, came to the house and said she had somebody she wanted me to meet. That was either a hit or miss with Leila. It could be a rap star or it could be a vegan person that's into meditation; you never quite knew what it was at that time, but it ended up being Pac. He came to my man Dize's house, and I can tell you what he was wearing too. He had these blue jeans on with these cow print patches all over it, and he had this haircut with the 360-degree part. He looked so different from everybody in my neighborhood, and I was trying to figure this dude out. She tells me, "This is Tupac and he rocks too, and I heard him rap and I told him about you guys, and I knew that I had to connect you two." So, there we were, and he was looking at us kind of strange, and at the time I was B-Boyed out. I wore my cap and it was tilted to the side with my belt buckle that said Roc-T, which was my rap name at the time, and I'm sure I looked strange to him. I asked him to rap for me, he did and I was blown away.

At the time, I was rapping about tennis shoes and girls, how dope my DJ was and how fly my fit was. I really wanted to be a rapper, but what he brought to my life was how powerful one single, solitary word can be. You take that word and you put it in the context of a complete thought, a complete structure of a song, and then people sing along to it and it becomes a part of who they are; it changes their outlook. It changes their DNA.

At the time, I didn't know that was what I was experiencing, but I realized how much I shifted in his direction as a writer. I started looking at my life. It was Pac's idea that we stop using monikers. So, we started using our real names. Pac was the one who called me Ray Luv initially, until it became a thing naturally. We decided to use our real names and tell our true stories and that was the beginning of everything. I had some success as a rapper and I was popular in my town, but when we started talking about real issues, I realized that everyone around me was going through the same exact thing, to some extent. That really was the genesis of it. That day we wrote five songs and recorded three. We started practicing for a show that very first day.

People always ask me about work ethic. My mother is Cab Calloway's daughter; she was also a performer along with my aunts. Work ethic was very high in my household, especially when it came to the arts and music. It was such an opportunity that you had to respect it, and Pac's work ethic surpassed my own. When I am not motivated these days, I think about what Pac would say if he was here. What would he say if I picked up the phone and called him, or if he came over and I was in my feelings and depressed? I know he would tell me, you have to get up and move. Nothing is going to come to a man on the couch.

Outside of his raps, he was a lot of fun. We had a lot of fun together. We probably did 100 hundred shows in 1988 and we didn't start at the beginning of the year. We really pushed a hard line. That was the beginning of it. We wanted to be in the majors. We didn't necessarily want to be on a major label, but we wanted to be a major voice for those who didn't have it. Even at that time, most of the people around us didn't have a voice.

Around 1989, Leila introduced us to Atron Gregory, the road manager for J.J. Fad at the time. He worked at Ruthless, right under Jerry Heller, and so, when we first heard about it, we thought we were going to be on Ruthless Records, and we were really hyped and running around telling everyone that we were going to be on Ruthless Records. That is what we thought we wanted at the time. In actuality, he had a smaller label called TNT Records, and on the label was Digital Underground and a hodgepodge of different groups that actually were a lot more alike in personality than we were in artistic expression. It came out differently, but there was a lot we had in common. When we connected with Shock G, Money B, Fuze and those guys, they were what we wanted to be. They were a few steps ahead of us at that time. We would go to the house in Oakland and it would just be twenty young rappers, musicians, DJs and everybody in one house creating one product. You hear about Motown and they had a system. You hear about Dr. Dre and the chronic and you hear how it was a group effort. We made records in those days as a collective. Parliament Funkadelic was the model for Digital Underground in terms of artistry, and that was our introduction to the game. We would do twenty-four-hour recording sessions. The sessions would run about $3500/day including the engineer. We would come there ready, and if you were off one day, you had to make sure you were on the next day. In that process the way Strictly Dope functioned as a unit was about getting the job done. So, as a group, when one of us needed something, we all put in effort. When we went into the studio to record music, depending on what was up next, it depended on how much effort everybody put into that one thing. There were times when Fuze played the drums and Shock came in and played keys; Pac wrote and wrote and wrote as long as he could write, and when he got tired, I wrote for him, and then I would write and write and record. When I got tired, he wrote for me. It's bits and pieces, here and there and everywhere. It was all created as a collective.

2Pacalypse Now is actually a fractured record of two different time periods meshed into one record. You have the 1989 portion of it and then you have almost a full year later completion of it. Tupac was much more candid and much more of an open book than most of us, and I remember at that time, being eighteen, I wrote a song that later was included in the album. It was called "Trapped." This was a song I wrote about the things I was going through at the time, but I wasn't ready to deal with it. I ended up ripping it out of my book and throwing it in the trash, and when Pac came in, he caught a small glimpse of it in the trash can and pulled it out and read it. He said to me, "Why did you throw this away?" I told him it was too personal. He told me, "Naw, nothing is too personal. That's the point!" So, we ended up having a whole conversation about it, until I was tired of talking about it and just told him that if he liked the material, then he could have it. He was down with that and he completed the song. Tupac never let a good verse, hook, or anything go to waste. He believed in rocking everything, and if it didn't work right now, then let's wait and it would work in the future.

Looking back on our journey, I understand that we weren't led in the best direction. I personally felt manipulated. We were eighteen and nineteen years old and understanding the dynamics of the business now, there are so many people who expect you to be an adult and move like an adult, but at that time, we were still kids. It was established that we would be separate entities and perform as separate entities even though we were under the same label and the same manager and, mind you, I signed my contract as a minor. I forged my signature because I was the only one who couldn't get my contract signed. It was easier for me to get out than for Pac to get out, and Pac was a loyalist. That led into a situation where there was a divide. I started noticing that when we were at the same shows and in the same places, we were divided. We would see each other, but as things got more serious, the more divided things got. In the early days, when we met Yo-Yo, those were really amazing times, and I wish I had a better perspective on our power, because we really did have the power to make all the decisions. However, we didn't know that, and if you don't know that, then other people make decisions on your life and it ends up the way it ends up. For me, I ended up going independent, and I signed to a label at the same time that he signed to Interscope. Despite the division and taking separate paths, we always stayed in contact with each other. I remember when he called me at some of his busiest times. He called me the day of the "California Love" video, in the middle of everything. The energy that he had at that time reminded me of how we were in the beginning. That feeling of having nothing to lose. Our best art came from when we felt that we had nothing to lose, and that's when we were the most honest.

Around the time of Pac's first shooting, we had just done two videos. We did these videos in the same weekend, and it was a special time period. It was almost a throwback to the old days. When we first started out, it was a beautiful experience. We brought the whole family together. The Thug Life crew, my crew, all the old school people came out to the video, and we shot these two videos. One of the videos that we shot, which was mine, the treatment called for old people, so we dressed up like old men, and now, as an adult, I realize that this was the only time that I got to see him as an adult. So we were dressed up and we were shooting the video and he was stressing out and I got to know something that the other guys didn't know, which was that he was going through a bunch of cases at the time and it was really a horrible time for him. I also was going through a lot at the time and as we were sitting together, I asked him, is it worth it? Is everything that we're going through worth it? He turned to me and said, "I absolutely think it is. I get up every day and I act as if, and I move as if, because it has to be worth it and has to make a difference." That type of certainty is something that I remember when I don't feel motivated. I get back to the basics of staying focused and I realize that I got that from this rebel, who taught me to understand that whatever your circumstances are, you can turn that around. How to get up and start moving, and when you start moving, other people start moving with you, and then it becomes a movement.

There is a book in Harvard that is about social activism in the modern era and our verses from "Panther Power" are in this book. To get through this advanced English course, you have to read this book. There are so many universities that I have had the privilege of speaking at and people I was able to connect with based on the things he and I wrote together. The macro of it is, Pac said that he would spark the brain that changes the world, and that is an understatement. He sparked so many brains in so many ways.

Judge Joe Brown said he became a judge because of Geronimo Pratt. His view was, if they could do Geronimo like that, then I want to be a judge to protect us. There are so many people who became judges all the way to moguls to people in the fashion industry and they are all being influenced by the same individual. I think that Pac gave complete and total honesty. As honest as you possibly can be. I think that is the secret sauce of Pac. You get where he is at right now.

Sometimes that is to the good. Sometimes you may not feel good about it, but you always knew where you stood with him, and even in branding, that kind of trust is what makes a brand viable. People trust that when they buy a Tupac record, it is authentic and it is not detrimental to Black people and it is about change and growth and pulling yourself up. For that I thank him.

He influenced my kids indirectly. My family was separated and for a long time, my little brother, who is fifteen years younger than me, and I weren't allowed to see each other. He was allowed to listen to Tupac's records and it actually came full circle and brought us back around. He found me because of my connection to Pac. I've had conversations with people who were trying to decide what they wanted to do and they revealed to me that even their family members would make statements such as "What would Tupac do?" I believe those stories because I have seen them. I have seen how one person starting a movement leads other people to move with you and it becomes a movement. There are people I know who refuse to work with you if you didn't support Pac.

When he died, I remember that me and the homies didn't listen to anybody else. If it wasn't us, then we weren't rocking with it. To the good or to the bad, however you felt about it. He brought that level of loyalty out in people. There was a time when he was at my house and two of the youngsters from my neighborhood, one Black and the other Mexican, got jumped by a group of college white kids. One of them was beaten up pretty badly. Pac didn't know them; only I knew them. I let them come in and Pac asked them what happened and they explained they got jumped. Immediately, Pac jumped up and said, "We're going to find the people that did that to your face." The whole group just followed him out the door. Instantly, the general in him, the spirit in him, he had no choice but to move how his spirit moved.

So, we went looking for the people who jumped them. We found them, and it was like thirty to forty people, but there were only six of us. When the police came, they lined the six of us up, and you had thirty to forty people pointing fingers and Pac said, "You're gonna line six Black kids up and let a crowd of white people say we did these things? That isn't even us. I just came off tour." And he started showing them pictures from the tour and jumped into this whole routine and got them to back off of us.

Afterward I asked him, "Where did you pull *that* from?" He says, "The white boy was about to point to you and say that you were the one that hit him. I had to show it and stop it from happening."

My relationship with Pac is about more than music. We recorded a few songs, but the basis of our relationship was true friendship. I had a really rough family situation at home and I left home really early, around fourteen or fifteen years old. I was homeless and sleeping in laundromats, and when I met Pac, he said, "I want you to come back to my house with me," and he lived in Marin City. My neighborhood was in Marin City, most of the people were related, sometimes we got along, sometimes we didn't. I said, "I don't think I'm allowed in Marin City; that sounds dangerous for me." He said, "No, don't worry about it. If they get you, they gotta get both of us." That was the first day I met him. That was the beginning of our friendship.

When I had problems with my older brothers and they would beat me up and abuse me, he would be like, "Nah, fuck that, we gonna go jump them." The crazy thing is, he was short and I was skinny. We weren't ready for war yet, but the heart was there; the caring was there. The empathy was there.

So, today I will argue and fight you over Pac. I don't know the Shakur's in any other way. It doesn't have anything to do with music.

Take that off the table. Just as a human being, and it taught me how you are supposed to handle a real friend. I didn't have a lot of good friends. He was the realest, and the world is a little dimmer without him. You can say that he is not the greatest, but I know a lot of rappers who took bits and pieces of him, from his raps to his swag to his energy, and there is no comparison.

Tupac's mom, Afeni, used to say that we were creating Black history, and when I look back over my life, I realize how many times I was a part of Black history. We performed at the Palladium in LA when we were very young. We had just met Yo-Yo and she just did her first tour, and we went to her apartment and hung out for a weekend. That weekend played a part for thirty years of my life.

We went and saw Jada and we also met Mike Tyson. That night we took a picture, and we were all young and hungry. To get into the club, we both signed our name under Trouble T Roy, who had just recently passed, and Pac was there when he passed. Mike Tyson says that picture of all of us hangs in his house and he remembers it as this amazing moment, and it really was. It was an amazing time period artistically. How it branched off to all these different ways and how all these different careers came out of that time period. A very small group of people that really just believed in what we believed in.

When you get older, the younger ones laugh at you because you say that Tupac is the best. I'm not saying that Tupac is the best, in the same way that people say that Nas is the best or Biggie is the best. What I am saying is that if you spend a twenty-four-hour period with this man and these people, you're going to walk away and say what I am saying. Pac was way ahead of his time. Especially with the urgency of someone who anticipated his life being short. At the time, a lot of us felt that we weren't going to live to see eighteen or twenty-five, but most of us said it yet lived as if that wasn't necessarily so. He, on the other hand, took action behind his belief. He believed that to be so and he put a level of urgency behind it.

There was a time we were all at this party that ended at about four a.m. You could not tell me that he wasn't at the party, and yet when it was seven in the morning, he showered and got up running around, telling us to get up and get things together. You believing he was at that party was just an illusion. His body was there but his mind was already asleep, in preparation for three or four hours ahead. He already was prepared to take that kind of action, and there is a lesson to learn from that.

THUG LIFE to me is a living document, and it is in recognition of where we have been, where we are at, and, if we are not careful, where we are going. A lot of the men were removed from our communities. There was a lot of separation within the Black families during that time. We were raised possibly not receiving all the love that we could have, and that is why we love so hard on our babies, on our kids now. There is still a deficiency. Collectively we still have not done enough. He said that if we are not careful, we will raise a nation of babies that hate the ladies that make the babies. Over time I have seen that more. The culture itself is different. The value of a life and friendship and loyalty and what honesty means and what family means is so distorted at this point, and if we want to reverse it, we have to go back to the basics, to the things that he was screaming fire about twenty-five, thirty years ago. To me that is a living, breathing thing. It's a verb, not a noun. It's something that we still have to address. It still has not been successfully addressed or handled. That is what it means to me. I have six friends who have lost their sons over the last four to five years. Young sons, all of them weren't in the street. Some of them were on their way to college;

256

some of them were doing other things. They were part of things all across the board.

We have allowed a climate to be created. Pac felt like everybody's kid was his kid, and he was going to take care of everybody's kid as if they were his own, and because we didn't do enough of that, we have a whole, generational community full of the devaluing of life. He left us bread crumbs to lead us in the right direction. He changed his way of living in order to create a space where young people could see him as a safe space. He showed us how to have love for one another. He said it is true that this is a crime land and a criminal world that we live in right now here in America, but when I talk to young people around the world who were one or two when he passed, or even those who weren't around at all, they say they are still inspired by him to be better. Children in other countries that I talk to tell me that their patron saint, their being able to overcome is Pac. That is not a fluke. There is a documentary about Palestine and Israel and the Palestinian children have posters of Tupac on their wall. He spoke to the desperate. The ones who are blessed have a responsibility to protect them.

RAY LUV
RECORDING ARTIST

RICH NICE

"He eloquently found a way to put the Black struggle in layman's terms so you didn't have to get super philosophical. You didn't have to get the long Malcolm X speech, although I love those, and you didn't have to get the long Martin Luther King "I have a dream" speech, and I love those. He was able to give it to you in three minutes of a song that made you see that's the real thought."

I FIRST MET PAC ON THE PUBLIC ENEMY TOUR, AND I WASN'T ON the Public Enemy tour. I was supposed to be, but, thanks to Motown, I wasn't; I was instead on the Motor Town review. Chuck D had invited me to come and do some spot dates on the Public Enemy tour. I was told that it might be better for me to do the Motor Town review. Marvin Gaye had the great Motown acts; I was thinking how that might be cool. I was also wondering who would be headlining. I was told The Boys, and I thought, where is Johnny Gill? I'm thinking that's not good for me, because their demo is fourteen to twenty-one and my demo was eighteen to thirty-four. That means I will be performing for little girls. I was made aware that Today was on the tour and the Good Girls. I agreed to the Motown Tour. Fast-forward, we're pulling into LA, the Hyatt on Sunset. The Public Enemy tour is there and they are about to pull out. When we pull up, we go in and we're talking in the lobby. The two tours pass through the lobby. I can see DJ Fuze, who DJs for Digital Underground. DJ Fuze and I had met at the conventions we had back in the day. We became friends and stayed friends, and so when I saw him in the lobby, we were excited to see each other. I said, "Come on my bus; I want to play you the remix." He grabs Money B and introduces us. Me and Money B start talking, and then Money B begins to ask, who do I look like? He thinks I look like Pac. They tell me that I have to meet Pac. Money B sent someone to go and find Pac, and they couldn't find him. We all went back to listen to the remix. They still could not find Pac. This was back when Shock G used to make people think he and Humpty were the same person. He would leave the hotel, dressed as Shock G, and they had to leave together, so his brother was dressed up like Humpty. He was going to light some fireworks off in the middle of Sunset in front of the Hyatt Sunset. I'm assuming he did that on a regular basis, whenever they left a hotel. Someone advised him not to do it and had the police come. They said that if you light those fireworks, we will not be able to get out of here and the police will go crazy. We are talking about the LA police in the early '90s, so you knew what that was going to be. He didn't light them. Shock G goes into the lobby and he starts playing the piano. Everyone gathers at the piano with him. The Good Girls are coming in with their bunny slippers on. All of the Public Enemy tour leaves and Digital Underground is the last to leave. Somebody said, "You have to meet your twin." Pac arrives. We take one look at each other and start laughing. It was a weird meeting because we met and we became friends instantly. As far as the music, it was the Digital Underground song that he was featured on, "Same Song." When I saw the video, I was jealous of his African joint. Later on, I heard that he hated it. He looked happy as hell. I wanted to do it and I was mad that you got to do it and I didn't, and he said I did it for you. I met him first and I heard the song after.

He had such a big platform; like Digital Underground, he was set up to do anything he wanted to do. He could have easily come back with a pop record and went straight to pop radio and been off to the races. He chose to make social commentary music. It made sense to me because my first album was called *Information to Raise a Nation*. I was pleased that we were in the same space. This was around the time everybody was telling me to get away from conscious stuff because you can't save the world. You can't save everybody, get out of that, and go do some radio records. Watching him stay in it like, "Brenda's Got a Baby." People said he will never be on the pop chart. I felt like he didn't need to be on the pop chart; you don't think that song is important? My boy had mixed reviews from people because they would always be like you can't save the world; it's like that's crazy that you feel that way because you don't think that information is going to help somebody? It was good to see someone that I knew, not that I didn't know, that liked the same things that I like, that like girls as much as I like girls, running around having fun, wilding, and everything. He was still able to sit and speak about how things aren't right. If we talk about things that are not right and we put messages out there that inspired me to stay where I was, I didn't feel alone.

If you are an educated person, the things he said hit home. Even if you didn't know everything, you were aware of what he was saying. Some of the kids in the projects, or some of those kids that are street kids or that might not have been on your front burner or even back burner and your family didn't care about that or even have that sort of information. He was able to tell you in the midst of what you wanted to hear. He was able to sneak a message in there. You weren't just going to be drinking and smoking listening to Public Enemy. They felt like you shouldn't be doing that; you almost had to be perfect. His music left you the affordability to have faults and still be Black. You could still be aware of what's going on, in your faults. You know that I'm not perfect, you didn't have to be perfect, but you could still be aware of what's going on. You don't have to be perfect to know that police brutality is wrong. The fact that you're not perfect doesn't mean that you get a pass to whoop my ass. Through his music and activism, he showed that I don't have to be perfect, nobody's perfect, you don't get to condemn me and beat me up 'cause I'm not perfect.

He said, "I might not change the world, but I will spark the mind that will change the world." That is the heavy part because it's people who didn't like rap and all of a sudden, Tupac's my favorite rapper. They don't like rap but like him. I don't know if it was the movies that sucked them in, but whatever it was, he was able to get certain people to like him. "Dear Mama" was a good song. You need a song like that. That was one of his major fingerprints on not just Black culture but on pop culture. Some of the most (for lack of a definition), anti-Black power movement people, like Tupac, do you know what he's about? Do you know his background? I don't know any of that; I just like him in that song, and I like his movies. This is coming from a white dude that doesn't really care, not that he's anti-Black, but he's not sitting there going Black lives matter, let's go, let's go...or Black power. But they like Tupac and will defend him. "Tupac is better than Biggie; I don't care what you say." You really rooted for Pac, and that's not even your world. That was his impact, to be able to convert people into having a Black consciousness without having to feel like they were embedded in Black culture. You can still have a Black consciousness without being embedded in Black culture.

My favorite Pac story, I have to go to the movie set of *Juice*. When he was filming the movie *Juice*, after a long period of time, I hadn't spoken to him. He had some success at this time. If you don't see someone in a while, you don't know what's going on with them. I was in the studio in the Bronx and Beast from Classic Concept called me. He said I should come by the set. They were filming *Juice* and your twin brother is the lead. I started laughing and said, "What are you talking about?" My boy said, "Who's that?" I told him who it was and that we should go down there. He said we should go right now without finishing the things we had going on in the studio. We all go down to Harlem, and when we get there, it's a girl with a walkie-talkie. I explain who I am and who invited me to come. She took me to a holding area where there were extras. I'm just there, thirty minutes went by, forty-five minutes. I saw this girl I knew, and we exchanged small talk. I got on the phone and called my boy who invited me there. He comes and gets us and takes us to this other place. This was the "VIP" holding area, because Omar Epps' group was there. Omar was in a singing group and the other members of his singing group were there. It's not super crowded like the extra area; this was another place, and was cool. This place had better drinks. Pac was in the middle of a scene and when they finish that, he will know you're here. In my mind, I wonder if he remembers me. Someone comes and grabs Omar's group and he says to me to come on. We're all walking to the set and Pac is coming out of the trailer. He looked, did a double take, and then he grabbed me. We started cracking jokes and walking and talking. He had to go and get ready to shoot a scene, the elevator scene. He wanted me to come with him. I went with him and tried to walk in and the man said, "You can't go here." Pac turned around and said, "He is with me, man." We start walking and now we're in the building. I didn't go with the idea of being in the movie. I had the idea to just hang out. Pac wanted us to stay with him. There was a little hallway with a camera and a light. The directors were there in front of me and I'm in the back. It was a girl, some sort of production assistant. Pac is talking with the director, talking about whatever with the scene, and the girl said, "You look just like Pac; is that your brother?" Literally, Pac turns around and goes, "Yeah, that's my brother; don't you see we look exactly alike?" Thus began the rumor in New York that me and Tupac were brothers. This girl ran her mouth that Tupac and Rich Nice are brothers. I'm laughing to myself because I don't know how long these shenanigans will go on. This girl had never said more than two sentences to me. Now, all of a sudden, I'm Pac's brother and she was into me. I see Pac talk to the director and point back at me. This is the scene where they're throwing the rent party, with the Quaker Oats box at the door. He pulls the dude off of that and sits me there. So I'm thinking, "Oh whoa, whoa, I'm in the chair." I start fixing my hat, getting ready to show I'm okay to shoot. Pac said, "He needs a line." They started thinking of what I could say. "The party's inside; the party's inside." People were in the hallway; the party's inside. They did the scene. Omar comes off of the elevator and Pac takes Omar and throws him on me. I fell to the ground. If you look at the movie, I crawled past the screen. It's just me and the screen. I got the closeup. They were doing the party scene inside the apartment; then it went to the roof. It's all about to be over, and Pac said they don't need him anymore, he is leaving. They said they need one person to say this line at the end; Pac grabbed me and told them that I have to say it. They didn't know the line so they huddled up together. Pac had gone back to the trailer. They huddled up together and came back and said the line is, "Now you got the juice." I thought we don't say that slang anymore, "Now You Got the Juice?" I didn't realize till later that the writers of *Juice* at that time were like fifty-year-old men. That's why they said that line, because that's what a fifty-year-old man in 1992 would say. We weren't talking that way, so I declined. They went back to the huddle again; they came back. That's the line, "Now you got the juice." I'm thinking in my brain, I'm on Motown records, working on an album. If I say, "Now you got the juice," I am going to look so wack. If anyone would say that, it would be a little kid. They let me know they would get someone else to say it. They grabbed the other kid, and he said, "Now you got the juice." If I had said that line, that would've been the memorable Rich Nice line of "Now you got the juice." I'm happy it didn't work for me. I left and told Tupac that the line didn't work. He started telling me a story, about how every day this dude is here hanging out with him. He doesn't have a job and he is down on his luck. He let him come hang out with him. They were eating, drinking, and smoking, when all of a sudden, his rings disappear and this nigga was nowhere to be found. Now he isn't here. The day he comes back, this nigga got on new sneakers when you told me you were down on your luck, you didn't have a job, you ain't got no money, my rings are here every day you here, and the one day you disappear, my rings disappear. Now you come back and you got new sneakers on. He started beating his ass. He felt like he couldn't trust people in his own trailer. He asked, "How am I supposed to trust my own Black people?"

When I first heard the term Thug Life, I was completely against it. This term is what we fight so hard to escape. I remember this girl's mother saying, "Don't be bringing them little thugs in my house." I'm like, "Are you talking about me?" I'm a nice guy, I have a mother and a father, I go to school, but then I had to look at myself in the mirror. I had cornrows, I was rapping, in the midst of the craziness, I used to wear spikes on my arms. From the outside, if you don't really know who I am, you will judge me as a thug. It made me think of how many people are judged as a thug from the outside, and you don't even know who they are. I had a homeboy named Howie. Howie was a bookworm. Howie was six three, big, and used to wear this army jacket, and this hat down low. Howie looked like a thug; Howie wasn't even a fighter. If I got into a problem, I wouldn't even say to go and get Howie to come and hold me down. I will tell Howie to stay home because you might get us beat up.

In the beginning, I didn't understand it, and I was kind of against it because I felt it was helping to dig a hole for us that we were trying to get away from. I started to really study it. You will call me that anyway. Thug Life is really the life of a person you imagine me to be. Even though I'm not what you think I am, that reflection of what you think I am, we will call it a thug. When I started to go to suburban places, this Thug Life concept is like a badge. A badge to make you back up; I don't really want no problems. Thug Life is an actual concept, to separate the real from the fake, because some of the rules are like no civilians. Immediately if you understand the concept of the streets, that's really what OGs did, except they didn't call it Thug Life. It was "street life," but the thing about that street life is, they are civilians. You don't include them in that, you leave them alone; street life had become so common and regular, watered down, that the term Thug replaced street. Street life doesn't mean anything, because if you are homeless, that's street life. Thug Life makes you understand that you have to have some morals about yourself, how to have a certain code to follow and not just be out here, crazy and wilding, because it's a code to everything.

He eloquently found a way to put the Black struggle in layman's terms so you didn't have to get super philosophical. You didn't have to get the long Malcolm X speech, although I love those, and you didn't have to get the long Martin Luther King "I have a dream speech," and I love those. He was able to give it to you in three minutes of a song that made you see that's the real thought. You can say what you want about him, but he is talking about realness. It made everybody think differently. Even in some of his MTV interviews where he talked about how you can't have a party next door and everybody is eating and throwing food around. The people on the other side of the door are hungry and starving. They will eventually stop knocking and kick the door in because it ain't fair. That sort of conversation in layman's terms from someone at that age, prepared everyone to understand you have to do something before it's too late. Things are going to change and either you help make the change or the change will happen and you won't even know it. You'll be left outside the door; that's the worst thing, for change to happen and you wake up and realize that everything has changed. What happened? You missed that boat; now you're playing catch up. You might not be able to catch up; you might be so far gone that that's it.

He also helped to cultivate Black thought, the inspiration of Black thought when it comes to thinking and being critical thinkers and intellectuals as Black people. We always feel like we have to make sure I get my Ph.D. before people will listen to me speaking anything that makes sense. He made it where you don't have to get a Ph.D. What I'm going to tell you is going to change your life one way or another. That's a big impact for the Black intellectual person with a Ph.D. You shouldn't talk down to anyone because they don't have a Ph.D. All of a sudden what I say is not valid because I don't have a Ph.D.? I'm a living Ph.D. My Ph.D. came from being in the actual streets and listening and talking to people, and seeing how it's affecting everybody. That's my Ph.D.

He was one of the best examples of the DIY movement because he always found a way to do it. Whether he had to partner with someone, he had a can-do attitude. He felt like it was always, we have to do something, we will not just sit still. That mentality is what made a lot of the younger guys of today look at him and respect him or like him more than some of the other people. In the beginning, it was so dope to see his rap style and talent just blossom. From when he used to double his vocals, I used to hate that. I watched him work to be better. I don't think the public has ever gotten to see someone grow in development in front of their eyes. Like when they heard Treach, Treach was Treach; when they heard Biggie, Biggie was Biggie; when they heard KRS, KRS1 was KRS1. They got to watch Pac's style evolve and change before their very eyes. I can't think of any other artist that we watched that way; it might've been some people that started one way and took a sabbatical and came back. Moment to moment, you got to watch him. He is the MVP; look what he's doing. He's not just getting better; he's also making people around him better and bringing people with him along the way.

He loved to party; I remember being in some dingy, dirty parties with him in Harlem. I would ask him, "Bruh, what are we doing here?" I'm thinking we would go downtown and he said, "No, we're Uptown." It was the strangest thing to me. It really made me understand how much he loved being Black. He could've gone downtown to any mainstream club and he chose not to. I loved it because that's where I was partying anyway. We had the green card to go. He wanted to hang out with his people. It was dope to see and feel that energy and be there and just be cool with what we were doing. We didn't care, and we didn't bring downtown up again for the rest of the night. Downtown was downtown and we were Uptown.

RICH NICE
HIP HOP IMPRESARIO

RUKIA LUMUMBA

"Tupac was able to speak a language
that people could hear and understand.
Tupac did that through his music.
He was unapologetically Black;
he was who he was. He wasn't scared
to be all of the ways we exist as Black
people. He was all of it. He represented
the best of us. He represented
some of the most challenging
experiences of us, representing it all."

THE BEGINNING FOR ME WAS WHEN WE WERE IN ATLANTA. IT WAS Black Nation Day. This was in the early '90s. It was before he came out with Digital Underground. It was a bunch of us, all of the New Afrikan Scouts, and a lot of Panthers. We were younger. I wasn't quite a Panther yet. We were in the basement and a lot of New Afrikans spent the night. It was a bunch of us, everybody you can think of. My parents were staying upstairs; Pac was staying there too. We were chilling downstairs, joking, playing games, and he said, "I'm 'bout to be famous." Everybody started laughing. He seriously said, "No, I'm about to be famous; I'm coming out with this new group." It was fun, one of those movement family times. We had so many growing up where you feel love, you feel comforted, and you feel like these are your people for life. He was there and he was one of them. It was a loving joke. When I got home to Jackson, Mississippi, a month later, I was watching Jukebox or MTV, a public access video channel. He was literally doing the Humpty Dance and I was like, "Oh My God, he was for real!" It was early in the morning; I ran into my parents' bedroom, and screamed, "Daddy! Pac is famous; he's on TV!!!" He said, "Girl, what are you talking about?" That was super exciting. I had never known any of us to actually be mainstream in any way. Not that time in my life. That really meant a lot to me because I felt we were always under the microscope, to be as New Afrikan as possible. We probably put ourselves under it, because of the movement. Not that other people weren't, but we were also under a microscope by our general community who thought we were weird for trying to build a Black nation. Having someone come from us that represents us be in the mainstream talking about the things we had been talking about. Not to be looked at as weird. He validated us. We were very lonely in Mississippi, where we were the only conscious family. I felt reassured; I felt like we are important, we exist, and that we are not different. We are building something for our people. It was my reality at that time and because of him, he validated a lot of what we were doing. As young people, the contradictions, tensions, and desires we had, outside of just what the traditional movement looked like, I appreciated that.

In Jackson, Pac had a performance at Tougaloo. I got in so much trouble that time that this is the one I remember. I got embarrassed real bad. He was performing at Tougaloo. Big, beautiful concert at Tougaloo; I was still in middle school. It was Black Nation Day again (always happens on Black Nation Day); my father worked out having him come to perform. I was asked to come backstage to say hey and just hang with him. I agreed. My mother already told me she didn't want me to hang with the older kids or hang with Pac backstage. She warned me not to go over there. She did agree that I could go to the concert. Walking toward the backstage entrance, there's a little barrier. My mother comes out of nowhere, right behind me, and snatches my arm. I didn't know it was her so I snatched it back. I pulled my arm back and, Lord have mercy, why did I do that? Pac was right there. My mother goes off in front of everybody and him and then snatches me up again and pulls me out of the concert. She took me back to the house and it was a whole thing. So that was my next time. Before that happened, he was like, "Ya know, little sisters, come on." He was pulling us back, and I know that he and my mother talked afterward. She was talking to the other adults at the table, (I was ear hustling); she was telling them she told Pac he has to pull it together. He can't be out here doing all these wild things, having these little kids following him like that. He can't be doing all of that and he listened. I'm happy he listened. She went on to say that he was a brilliant boy. In her conversation, she was feeling proud of him, at the same time, feeling like, I want to guide

274

you because I don't want you to get hurt. That was more of what she was saying more than anything. I don't want our children to think that doing certain things is the right thing to do. That was a continuation of everything that we have experienced as movement children, our parents trying to make us be better than the mistakes that they've made. Doing it in such a deep love and deep way of community. She didn't give birth to him, but she still felt like she had a responsibility to tell him what she thought was the right path to take. I appreciated that he was the topic of conversation in our house often when my father began to represent him. It was beautiful and it was hard; representing people through criminal cases is hard, especially when it's people you love. Not being able to control the narrative and not being able to control the person, either; you can't control people, period. You want it to be easy but it's not easy; you want everybody to show up in a way where people can't talk about them, but that doesn't exist. During the rape case, my father was very angry.

All of us felt so angry, and for my father, he felt that they had been through this before. You know better, you know what COINTELPRO is, you know all of this, you can't put yourself in these situations. As young people, you know that it's not enough to have been through it sometimes, it's not that easy, you can, not, put yourself in situations and still find yourself in situations because the situation comes to you.

He would call at different times of the night. Every time he would call, he would talk to us for a bit. He would ask how we were doing. What were we doing? What video games were we playing? He felt like a big cousin and made you feel like you were a part of his life. He was definitely a part of all of ours. There are so many people he doesn't even know; as I got older in high school, we always had

275

people living with us. One of my closest friends, who lived with us, was one of his biggest fans. She loved him so much; she never got to meet him. She had the whole locker filled with his pictures. When he passed, we all took it hard, but it was so many people he never met that grieved as if they have known him his whole life. She definitely was one; it impacted her for a long time, it impacted her being. Even with her grades, everything. It was through his music and through his interviews that she had seen him.

Honestly, he is one of the sole reasons why we have a Black Lives Matter movement now. They say Fred Hampton, Sr. was able to connect with the community and speak a language that people could hear and understand. Tupac did that through his music. He was unapologetically Black; he was who he was. He wasn't scared to be all of the ways we exist as Black people. He was all of it. He represented the best of us. He represented some of the most challenging experiences of us, representing it all.

He had just come out with Thug Life and bought all of these shirts and hats for everybody. He explained Thug Life to us. He explained to us what niggas mean, never ignorant about getting goals accomplished. Our parents had an issue with why we were wearing that. I was wearing it proudly. Thug Life connected to that, meaning freedom to win. In one of the interviews he did, at the Malcolm X Center in Atlanta, he talks about it. Everything that he represented for us, and everything we had talked about in passing in small conversations. All that he was talking about in his music and Thug Life, niggas, and all of that, was literally about how we develop our own power. Thug Life is about how we really fulfill the mission of our parents around our liberation and creating safe spaces for our people and a better quality of life. Thug Life meant that you were down in any way to make sure that happened; you were committed to our people, to our liberation, and understanding that our liberation meant that we deserve good quality and better quality of life. The power to determine what that looks like and to govern ourselves.

It's a feeling but also a conscious understanding that he opened the way for us to connect our theory with where our people are in terms of the conditions that we are experiencing. He told the story so accurately, you can't deny that we are going through it. He laid out a blueprint through his music and his poetry, through his being and his interviews. He laid out a blueprint for us around this. He laid out this blueprint on what it is to be young, Black, and liberated. Liberated in our own person so that we could actually build toward the dreams that we have, not just talk about it. Not just in our inner circles, he dared us to move beyond people who thought like us. To move deeper into our communities, to learn from exactly the same folks that are our neighbors, that are our loved ones, that may not think like us, they may not use the same language, but they definitely have the same goal. We often get in a space where we are holier than thou as New Afrikans sometimes. We think that we are better than folk who aren't us. That's problematic, not building. He recognized that and he moved in that way, which showed me that I can do anything. Not to be scared of what people will think. Don't be scared about whether you will actually succeed or make it because you will. You just need to know it can happen. He's an example, you are an example, there are so many examples of who didn't follow the path of our parents. You followed a different path; you went beyond what they had laid out for us and took us to a next level. He was a part of that crew that did it. You all have done that for us (referring to Aiyisha and Chaka Zulu). There's no way Chokwe Antar would be mayor had y'all not already laid the foundation around what was possible for us. Being greater than what our parents were able to do in their lifetimes. He made everybody feel like you knew him real well. He was amazing. He put us on the map; he exposed what we were doing to the rest of our people in the nation; he made it all right to be affiliated; he made it feel more welcoming.

RUKIA LUMUMBA
LEGAL ADVOCATE AND ACTIVIST
EXECUTIVE DIRECTOR, PEOPLE'S ADVOCACY INSTITUTE

SHANTI DAS

"It's like Tupac had a crystal ball looking into the future to see some of the things that were going to continue being the plight of our community."

IWAS FIRST INTRODUCED TO THE MUSIC OF TUPAC AMARU SHAKUR from listening to it on the radio back in the day. I remember being a young girl at the time. I learned more about him when I was in college. He was on the road with Digital Underground and started gaining notoriety. I was a radio disc jockey at Syracuse University and we started playing a lot of his earlier material.

When I was a student at Syracuse, I joined a couple of different groups and organizations. While going to a predominantly white university, I was always very conscious of my Blackness. Early on, Tupac made party records; most importantly, he made records about society. In the early '90s, when I graduated, I felt he was speaking to us. It was very refreshing to hear a young rapper talk about what Black people went through in society. He pushed societal norms, and that is what I appreciate about him and his music.

One thing that is really compelling for me is that Tupac was *Black Lives Matter* before the movement was even thought about. Twenty-five years before it came to fruition in our culture, he talked about Black people being in prison and the dislike for police. The spoke of how this has manifested in our society. In the last five or six years of police brutality, many African-American men are getting killed by cops. It's like he had a crystal ball looking into the future to see some of the things that were going to continue being the plight of our community. His activism was alive and well throughout his music in songs like "Changes" and so many other of his incredible songs. He was ahead of his time. He was a visionary, and a leader in every sense of the word as a Black man in our society.

In a more personal approach, it was his kindness. For those who had the good fortune to meet him in person or come across him in real life, he was as real as it gets. If he was your friend, he was your friend. I didn't talk to him on the phone; however, anytime I saw him (from the first time we met), he was kind and gracious. He gave me a radio drop for my station when I was in college. Once I was working in the entertainment industry and became a high-level executive, he always stopped and greeted me with a smile and a hug. Tupac always showed me the utmost respect. I appreciated his humanness and kindness. Over the years there was controversy with music, lyrics, and the man Tupac, but he *really* was a good guy. He embodied kindness, and there was another side of him I knew wasn't all about the rah-rah. He was a gentle person, and consistent. He was the same every time I saw him. I appreciated that about him, especially in the entertainment business when things aren't always consistent or people aren't always consistent.

It was 1991 or 1992, I was in Washington, D.C. as a college student going to a hip-hop conference called The Cultural Initiative. I was standing in the lobby by myself so I could network and try to meet people in the entertainment industry. At that time, I was trying to find my way into the business. I saw Tupac walk across the room and I was like, "Oh My Gosh, That's Tupac. I am going to go up to him." He was traveling with Digital Underground. He was working on a lot of his own things. I walked up to him and said, "You don't know me, but I have a college radio station show at Syracuse University; I would love to have a drop from you." He was kind and he did it for me. I wish I still had the tape. He went on to ask: How are you doing? What is your name? Where are you from? What are you doing at the conference? I told him I was just trying to network and meet people. It happened to be my birthday that day and he said, "Well, it's your birthday, what are you doing to celebrate your birthday?" I told him, nothing, and I'm really just here to work. He told me I couldn't be by myself on my birthday and let me hang out with him and his crew. We went to some shows and it was the best day of my life. I was a kid in a candy store, so excited that Pac actually let me hang out with him. Ever since then we were cool. One time, I had been in the industry for quite some time and was making a name for myself; I went to a radio show on the West Coast and it featured Tupac. I was walking backstage to go outside to my car and I saw him and his crew in their white van pull off. He made the driver pull back around and stop; he got out to give me a hug, got back in the car, and drove off. He did that just to say hi and give me a hug. That's who he was.

My interpretation of Thug Life is the hate spewed within America to young Black and brown babies shaping our future. When you hate on babies, you are having a detrimental effect on their livelihood. You're traumatizing children right when they come out of the womb. We hear about discrimination in our underserved communities and it is real. It's about opportunities and exposure. If we didn't give so much hate to our young Black and brown kids, they would have the same opportunities that young white and Asian kids might have. It's biblical, because we've seen it since the beginning of time. Often, we see how the cops treat our young Black boys and Black girls, and everyone expects so much from them in society when you're stunting their growth out of the womb. There is no even or clean slate at the beginning of their lives. They come into this life with a mark on their forehead because they are Black. You have to have a strong family support system, a strong spiritual system, and, unfortunately, everyone does not have the support system around them. Some of these kids do not have the same opportunities or resources available to them. There are many socioeconomic issues and social determinants in our communities. It gets tough for Black and brown kids to get ahead because we are not given a fair shot. Tupac knew this, talked about it, and was unafraid. That's what I loved about him. You might get a party record from Pac, but you're also going to get the realities of what is happening in our communities. He had a special anointing on his life.

Tupac prepared us for the world today by not being afraid to talk about the wrongs in our society. Holding police and people that continuously contribute to the plight of the African-American community accountable. He held their feet to the fire and he wasn't afraid to speak up and share his thoughts. He paved the way for activism, especially in music, and we see it in music artists and actors who have joined the movement. Those who have stepped up and stood out from an activism perspective. He and Public Enemy led the way and were leaders in this space for our community. They made it cool and talked about being in the club but also about police brutality.

SHANTI DAS
MUSIC INDUSTRY VETERAN
FOUNDER OF SILENCE THE SHAME

SHERI RILEY

"You can be Black, and powerful, and have a little rebellion to you."

IWAS INTRODUCED TO TUPAC'S MUSIC WHEN I WAS IN COLLEGE. AT this time, music was dominated by N.W.A., X Clan, and Public Enemy. Digital Underground came on the scene with this fun energy. Then Tupac dropped his first album and I was like, "YO, this is something different." It was such a contrast from what he was doing with Digital Underground. Coming into my own awareness in college, the depth of his words and storytelling, as well as the rhythm and flow, immediately catapulted him to being one of my top artists. I'm from Kentucky, and during this time, there was this evolution in my own personal mindset, cultural awareness, and understanding of what it meant to be Black. Tupac had this fire about him and he was so rhythmic. I appreciated him as an artist because his music was good, the energy was great, and his message spoke to this young twenty-something-year-old, trying to figure out her own journey. I could ride around grooving to the music, and there was this message that made me feel there's a little rebellion in me, as well. For a young college student, who was finding her own voice, he empowered me to understand that you can be Black and powerful and have a little rebellion to you.

SHERI RILEY
EMPOWERMENT SPEAKER
HIGH PERFORMANCE LIFE COACH
AWARD WINNING AUTHOR OF
EXPONENTIAL LIVING

STEPHEN HILL

"At a time when many were trying to say all the right things, Tupac was going to give the truth, and I appreciated that."

TUPAC SHAKUR FIRST HIT MY RADAR WHEN I WAS THE PROGRAM director for WILD radio Boston. I was a huge Digital Underground fan from jump; literally, *Sex Packets* is one of my top-ten hip-hop albums of all time. I often feel like I'm the only one waving THAT flag. Then, on the EP following their first album, they brought in this guy named Tupac. The DU universe was paying attention. That's how I was put onto him.

To me, Tupac was among the very first youth who was into using lyrics to provoke thought and activism. Chuck D always felt like he was an adult; a grown-ass man. Chuck always felt like he was speaking from a place of authority. When Chuck first hit on the scene, you felt like this brother got it all figured out. Tupac was figuring it all out *with* us and was extremely adept at articulating our struggles. He's along for the ride; he's making mistakes and figuring out as he goes, but with that razor-sharp mind. He was able to take data from situations from our society and process it in an effective way that people of his own generation, of his age, could understand. People were looking up to him and even more effectively, people were looking *across* at Tupac when it came to how he impacted the culture.

Tupac was among the first multidimensional hip-hop figures. In early hip-hop, it felt like you picked a side. Are you "conscious?" Cool, that's your lane. Are you partying? Cool. That's your lane. Tupac was among the first to challenge your booty and your brains; you're gonna get "I get around"...and you're gonna get "Dear Mama" as well.

I gotta be honest: I am admittedly from the sidewalks and not the streets. Thug Life, to me and in my upbringing, was not the acronym Tupac intended: "The Hate U Give, Little Infants F&ks Everyone." "Thug Life" is a thing you didn't want any part of. Thugs are the people your parents worked endlessly to both keep you from and keep you from becoming. I appreciate the word "thug" and specifically it's redefinition. "Thug" is like "Nigga"; a word with which I reject association and at the same time I can respect how Tupac and his generation reclaimed those words in the way to give it power. I'm still not trying to be either one of those words, though I can appreciate how a new generation usurped the words.

The first time I ever met Tupac was on a press junket for *Poetic Justice* when I was at that radio station in Boston. The movie company brought journalists to a hotel; we put all our recording devices on a table in front of him and we asked Tupac questions about John Singleton's film. I may have been one of only two Black people in the room. He was unbelievably eloquent and thoughtful in his responses. He spoke of what it meant to work with John Singleton and what it meant to work on *Poetic Justice*. There weren't that many questions about justice or things going on outside of *Poetic Justice*. To sum it up...Tupac is: eloquent and articulate. Damn. "Articulate." That's the one word you never want to hear white folks call Black folks. I prefer the word "eloquent." "Articulate" is like the bare minimum; he conjugates verbs and enunciates the correct vowels. When the round robin interview was finished, he got up to walk out...I grabbed my device (a mini-disc recorder!) and got next to him. I had heard the rumor that he had to take an HIV test before being able to kiss Janet Jackson (his co-star in *Poetic Justice*)...I HAD to ask.

"Hey, brother, I appreciate you, appreciate your music. Hey, is it true you had to take an HIV test to kiss Janet?" He turned and gave me a full-toothed smile. "Yeah, I had to take it. I said if we gon' really do it, then I will take the test. If we just gon' kiss, I'm taking no test." The PR person ran into the room and said we shouldn't have any more questions and it was time to go. Even when doing a press junket, when you're supposed to say all the right things, Tupac was going to give the truth, and I appreciated that.

292

Tupac is a prototype and a blueprint for young black thinkers and he shows the value in being multidimensional. You can go to the party and hang out on Saturday night and on Monday morning be trying to uplift your people through the word. Indeed, what we have to remember was that Tupac was only twenty-five when he passed. TWENTY-FIVE. Frontal cortex had likely not even closed yet. Look at the music he was making at twenty-one. One of the most amazing things about *Judas and the Black Messiah* is the reminder that Fred Hampton was twenty-one. That's how amazing Tupac was for a new generation using a nascent platform to move culture ahead. Stacey Abrams, Tamika Mallory, and all these folks standing on the shoulders of Tupac in terms of moving the people forward through word and deed.

Time has blurred some sharp edges of my memory. I was working at MTV in September of 1996 and I remember Tupac and Snoop Dogg walking down Fifty-First Street, turning left and entering Radio City Music Hall the night of the MTV Video Music Awards. I was assigned to Bone Thugs-N-Harmony that night. We always checked to see who had beef with whom to make sure that everyone kept the right distance and kept respect. Attempting to confirm a rumored beef, I asked the group if they had any issues with Tupac. Bizzy Bone said calmly, "Nah, we have no problem with Tupac,"... and then a little less calmly, he concluded with, "...unless he tries to start something." Tupac and Snoop Dogg walked down the carpet, and who knew that later that month, Tupac would be gone. He had charisma and is one of those people that walked in the room, and even without speaking, his presence was felt.

STEPHEN HILL, DUDE
RADIO AND TELEVISION EXECUTIVE

STOOP LAUREN

"People always think he's not a perfect role model, but he's a perfect role model for me."

I WAS A BABY WHEN PAC PASSED, MAYBE FIVE. IF I COULD REMEMBER anything, it was the conversations. Super big in different ways, he made me express myself genuinely and not hold back, not being fearful of what other people think about you, or even the work ethic, like how much you actually have to work. He influences me in so many different ways. To me he also affects people in a large way. If you notice, they use him as someone to kind of stand on top of because he was so public with how he felt, and not just only about what we're going through right now, but just like the system and bettering the community, and at the same time, he was popular, so it was like he was preaching two messages. He stands on both points firmly, and leads by example, so I just felt like he makes people feel more, like they use his voice to go, "You know what? I can do that too." It's almost like they are living through him and his image.

I feel like he was major like that because they don't reference people like that. No disrespect to other artists, but they don't go to Biggie, or Snoop, and those are my favorite artists, Jay-Z as well, but they go to Pac instantly. I feel like if he was in this era and he had YouTube, he would be the biggest ever. I love the movies *Juice* and *Above the Rim*. I love how he was able to study those characters and really hop into these people's shoes and express those neighborhood stories that you really don't hear about because it was painted a certain type of way, but it was like he's giving you his swag mixed with the story and how the movie was written. It was like, okay, this guy really has an understanding of people and how to convey certain emotions to get a reaction.

I love seeing him behind the scenes talking about what he's doing, and everything. I know about him through film and TV, so everything I see is how he presented himself, and he showed how brilliant his mind was. As far as when you talk about Thug Life, to me it is just a way of being strong. I feel like even in the corporate world, they play these societal games where they have these glass ceilings like on women, and on our people, Black people, but I feel like in those situations, even you could be Thug Life, corporate thuggin', or a female saying nope, there are no ceilings for me, and then boom! Take it to the next level and nobody stops you. Thug Life to me is everything; it's every day. He prepared you for the world because he told you what's going to happen if you don't change. When he was acting, you could feel that emotion. I want to say thanks to Pac for being a strong influence. I'm so thankful he was able to leave us strong, positive messages. Some people may think he's not a perfect role model, but he's a perfect role model for me.

JEFF DIXON JR.
AKA
STOOP LAUREN
ARTIST/PRODUCER

TAHIRA WRIGHT

"He had an effortless swag about him…
I mean the man was FINE! Besides that,
he spoke on real topics that affected
Black people on an everyday basis."

IWAS FIRST INTRODUCED TO PAC WATCHING MUSIC VIDEOS ON MTV, reading *VIBE* magazine, and through my peers. He was really popular when I was in junior high going into high school. I'm sure any boy I had a crush on listened to Pac, and he was just the embodiment of the culture. "I Get Around" had to be the first time I was captivated by Pac as an artist. He had an effortless swag about him...I mean the man was FINE! Besides that, he spoke on real topics that affected Black people on an everyday basis.

My favorite Tupac-inspired story is when you broke the Internet. You posted the photo on Instagram of Pac holding up his sweatshirt with "Thug Life" tatted. And who is in the photo, with hair down her back cascading ever so effortlessly? My sis Aiyisha. Now mind you: this is a photo of Pac, but I'm over here stanning and a huge fan, 'cause I'm like, "That's my sis! Do y'all see her in the picture?" And that's honestly one of my favorite moments! Because it was just a nostalgic moment in time, and it was a way to see what you had been telling me over the years about your relationship with him. It's organic, everyday, y'all hanging out and someone just happened to take a shot and that's just what it was. It's beautiful. So it's one of my faves because it involves you.

And just to have that moment captured in time, it lets you know how important photographs are. You know, with the social media era, I think sometimes people go overboard. But capturing those moments is important, because you can look back at it, your kids can look back at it. And it's like, "Yeah, this was like some real life that I was living out here!"

When I was younger and didn't know, I thought Thug Life meant, "We thuggin' out here in these streets!" I really thought that's what it was! Just 'cause you didn't know. And then he signed to Death Row, and we know the connotation behind a lot of that with the

Suge Knights of the world and all that kind of stuff. So that's what I thought it was. Until I would see interviews of him really talking about the youth, ultimately, and how they are groomed by society. Especially, let's be specific: Black youth and how they are NOT groomed by society and therefore grow up to just try to survive by any means. And talking about how poverty affects us and being disenfranchised and not having the same opportunities. Being discriminated against based on the color of our skin; which, you know, we thought 400 years of slavery was enough, but clearly, we're in 2021 and this is still going on. So just him taking that moniker—which I'm sure attracted the youth because that's what was attracting them—but really flipping it into something positive and trying to create a way for them. And to me, I think that that's something that needs to be implemented across the board today. 'Cause I'm not tryna call out any rappers, but you know: they're promoting a lot of drug culture, a lot of misogyny and different things. And I'm not saying that didn't exist then, but it's like, where's the balance, you know? And you see it in certain artists that are obviously, I'll say, "children of Pac," like the Kendrick Lamars, J. Coles, and Nipsey Hussle. Like, you see the descendants of Pac and people that take those messages forward; we're seeing more of that. But yeah, "Thug Life" flipped for me as I understood it more. I grew up and realized what he was really pushing behind that message. I'm not getting a tattoo with it, though. But much respect.

I think that if you listen to Tupac, you get a feel for what his messages were. I think some people, other people didn't want to hear what he was trying to really say, but now they're seeing it continuously play out. So he spoke nothing but the truth, if you were willing to listen, to hear, and not just talk and think that you knew what he was about because of maybe other records that you heard.

So yeah, it's…You know, I think it was one of the interviews I watched, I think it had to be MTV, and it was a forty-minute interview—the classic one where he has the striped jersey, Marlon Wayans is in it, and they're promoting the movie *Above the Rim*, which is another one of my favorites. But you know, he was just speaking the truth. And that's all I can really say about him: he was speaking the truth and what's real and he said that no matter what. No matter who he was talking to, no matter what arena he was in; that's what it was about for him. And he had it instilled in him from a young age.

I don't know; it's crazy because you try not to question God and why certain things happen. But it also makes you wonder, if Pac was here as a fifty-year-old man, what would that look like? What would he be doing? How would he continue to impact us? Would some of the ideas that he wanted to implement have been in full swing? How much more change could have been affected if he was still around? It makes you wonder. But then, it should also, like him and many other revolutionaries, make US feel empowered enough to say, "How can we continue that message? And how can we continue to fight for the betterment of our people?"

TAHIRA WRIGHT
FOUNDER & CEO, THE CUT LIFE

TERRI J. VAUGHN

"Tupac was a prophet, a storyteller, trailblazer, speaker of truth, and a God who spoke with a God-tongue. The truth sometimes hurts and sounds horrible, but it is still the truth."

IWAS FIRST INTRODUCED TO THE MUSIC OF TUPAC SHAKUR through Digital Underground. I'm from the Bay Area and Digital Underground was huge for us. Tupac was a big part of that. He was part of their dynasty. The song I love from Tupac is "I Get Around."

Tupac was brave, raw, and completely honest about his truth. Whether you agreed with him or not, he said amazing things through his artistry. He said things I absolutely loved and adored that were divine. He also said things that were harsh and scary at times, but it was his truth. His truth is what we could get behind. Music has much meaning and is powerful to our lives and different chapters of our lives. Tupac was always raw and honest. Anything lyrically he has ever said out of his mouth was all truthful for him. They were never things that were fraudulent or him acting or pretending to be something he wasn't. He was who the fuck he was, and that is a gift to the world. To be able to stand in your truth, right or wrong. Being honest to yourself. That is a gift. That is what we all aspire to do, to speak and be our truth. Tupac was definitely that.

Tupac was the voice of our streets and the voice of our culture. In speaking his truth, many of us could relate, which was huge for us. To be able to hear a voice that is speaking what we know, what we've seen, and how we feel. Tupac was unapologetic about it. He spoke with no fear against the backdrop of how our America is. He was like many other young artists. This is why we love rap and hip-hop, both unwavering in pointing out the wrongs of society. Calling out the police. Calling out the government. Calling out the system that is set in place. Tupac was an advocate for that and was living his life as a threat to the system. That is really what he represented for us and for the culture. He was not afraid to be a threat. It goes back to his upbringing and his family being dedicated to pouring truth into the lives of Black people and people in the ghetto. He carried that in his art, which is a beautiful thing. That is what art is supposed to do. Art is supposed to challenge us. Art is supposed to speak our truth. Art is supposed to make a change. And Tupac did it. He did it raw and sometimes mean, because that is what you have to be where we come from.

In the realm of hip-hop, Tupac will always be one of the greatest. He is the greatest not just because of words and truth; he was an artist as well. He was an artist in his delivery, his passion, and his excitement. Any artist, especially a hip-hop artist, would be an inspiration to your art, your artistry, in not making it sound like someone else and being its own thing and standing on its own. There was no one who was like Tupac. You would never hear a conversation where someone says, "Oh, he sounds like Tupac," or, "This reminds me of Tupac." It was his own voice, which was raw, and his passion was monstrous. In his passion, he spoke with fire. On the same note, he spoke with much love. That's the foundation of all of it. Because of his love for his people and himself, he was willing to put it all out on *wax* (as you would say back then). He put it all out there because he loved us that much. This story has to get out and it has to get out with desperation so the people will get the message. He knew when to push it and when it had to be pushed angrily and when it had to be pushed softly. He had a variety of different temperatures with his music and raps. A variety of temperatures with the love for his mother and the love of Black women. Curse you out and then understand your plight, which was just amazing. There are some amazing artists; however, you will never find anyone that sounds like Tupac. He did it the way he did it.

I was in college when I first heard about Tupac. We fell in love with him through his music, but when we saw him in *Poetic Justice*, the heart-melting happened. Growing up where I grew up, we were always attracted to the bad boys. Tupac was a bad boy in his music because of how raw, how broad it was, his ego, and all of it. We were already drawn to him then when he was in *Poetic Justice*. As an artist myself, watching him work as an actor, I was completely intrigued and blown away by the effortlessness of his work, the truth, and honesty. Also watching him and those eyes, smiles, laughs, and eyelashes, he melted my heart. I was like, "I wonder if I could be with him." I was impressed and blown away by him with the movie; he was amazing.

Thug Life means thuggin' it out. Making it by any means necessary. No matter where I come from, I'm going to push my desires and my voice forward. I'm going to make it happen for me and for the people. I'm going to thug this shit out. This is Thug Life for me. His life was in the hood where it took on the thug and ghetto mentality because that is where it was birthed. We were growing up in the hood trying to have things in life. We were trying to have success, money, finer things in life, and were going to push through and thug this shit out. Thug Life.

Firstly, Tupac was a prophet. While alive, he spoke to the time we were living in and how it was manifested and lived out in America and beyond. He spoke about the system and how things will continue to happen and continue to spread if something wasn't done about it. Most of his music spoke to this. Everything he talked about, everything he talked against, and everything he stood for—we are still living in this time in the worst way. There is power in being an artist and being connected to your source while speaking the truth from a place of purity of heart from which he spoke his truth from. His truth was pure and not made up. It was honest, and we are still living in that truth. This is sad and heartbreaking. Nothing has been fixed. Tupac was a prophet, a storyteller, trailblazer, speaker of truth, and a God who spoke with a God-tongue. The truth sometimes hurts and sounds horrible, but it is still the truth. That was his way of showing his love and leaving his legacy with us to this day. He called everything out. I wonder what his next level of truth-telling to help us would have been. He would not have held back. We must honor him. He was one of our gifts. His energy was infectious. Tupac represented the true spirit of an artist and what artists are supposed to use their gifts for. Whatever your gifts are, you are supposed to speak to and for the people.

TERRI J. VAUGHN
ACTRESS, DIRECTOR, PRODUCER

TUMA BASA

"Listening to Tupac's lyrics, he sounds like a prophet. In reality, he was just expressing what he saw. He didn't hold back. He had no fear in terms of what he said."

I THOUGHT I DISCOVERED TUPAC. I WAS IN ZIMBABWE AT THE TIME and my friend, General Ntshalintshali, lent me his *2Pacalypse* cassette, with no context of who he was. I assumed his name was pronounced "Two Pack" and it was a group because of Money-B's verses. I remember vividly listening to it for the first time. I was in my parents' room making their waterbed, blasting his cassette from my portable stereo. I just remember thinking, "This is really good." Around that time, I played "Brenda's Got a Baby" for my sister and she cried. To me, in my head, I discovered Tupac.

My friend the general ended up explaining to me that "Two Pack" wasn't a group and his name was pronounced "Tupac." I even ended up watching *Juice*. In the '90s, movies came to Africa slower than new music. I can honestly say that I am happy I listened to the music before I watched the movie. While I know that *2Pacalypse Now* isn't his greatest body of work, it's my sentimental favorite.

I met Tom Whalley years later, when he was the CEO of Warner Bros. I remember saying to him that if I was an A&R at the time, I would have signed Tupac too. Every time I discover someone's music organically, I always get that feeling again. That feeling when I was playing Pac's first album while I was making my parents' waterbed.

Another thing about Tupac is that his music was street and had a lot of edge, but at the same time, it had information density. It was emotional, but you always learned when you listened to his music. His ability to call out people and name names, such as George Bush and CIA and the police, was mind-blowing. He didn't care. He spoke his mind. He made sure to get his message across.

When I think of the impact of his music, I compare him to Bob Marley. Pac and Bob Marley are the two prototypes of artists who transmit "message" through their music. Bob Marley is the mellow vibe and Tupac is the hard vibe. They aren't the same, but the emotional response is the same. The same from those that seek information and higher understanding.

When Pac got too much into Thug Life, I actually stopped liking him. I was strong in my conscious mindset at the time, and with Thug Life, he started losing me. When his music and actions started to feel like theatrics, antics and performative, he started losing me. The Death Row era made me feel uncomfortable. Looking back, I understand that I was also in a time of growth. What I understand now about Thug Life is counter-society. It is more about energy. It is about picking yourself from the bottom. It's more attitudinal than it is musical.

Tupac's impact can be seen today in so many ways. For one, every rapper now has a song about their mom on their album. His "Dear Mama" is the standard for those songs. And there have been so many "mini-Pacs" since then. It's gotten to a point where a generation that wasn't even born when he was alive, recognizes images from classic Tupac moments and visuals.

I remember September 1996 vividly. I was transferring schools and I didn't say goodbye to my old friends from my prior school, I just left, so I went back to say bye properly and get my stuff. I couldn't afford a return flight from Salt Lake City to Iowa City. I could only afford one that got me to Kansas City and I bummed a ride from there with two friends. We found out Tupac had died right before we left KC, so the whole ride back was pure silence. We were shocked, in disbelief. Remember, this is 1996, so we couldn't just plug in an aux cord and play his music from a streaming service. Those days, you had to already have the CD in your car.

No one thought that Pac would actually die. It wasn't his first time being shot and he had survived before, so we thought, why wouldn't he survive this time? Unfortunately, he didn't. When Pac passed, I started reconnecting as a fan. I started digging in again. And for a good year after he passed, there was the discussion on whether or not he was faking his death. A lot of people didn't know how to process his death. Now we just celebrate the words of his life.

TUMA BASA
MUSIC/TECH EXECUTIVE

WATANI TYEHIMBA

"Imagine a fifty-year-old Pac; I see a much calmer, much more centered person. Still that "Pac" energy; I can see a fifty-year-old Pac and not a twenty-five-year-old. Today he would have a greater influence on not only the music but young people in general."

IT'S VERY INTERESTING THAT I HAVE NEVER BEEN ABLE TO LOCK down the age that Tupac was when I first met him. He was obviously a child in New York. We traveled back and forth. He was always there.

I know Mutulu and Afeni came to the West Coast right after his sister, Set, was born; I saw Pac somewhere in the early seventies. We would see him as a child traveling with all of us. Regular interactions. Traveling back and forth just seeing people at the events. When we were at a conference, he was always that child that stood out. You could see there was a difference there; he would command the presence of the room, as a youngster.

Pac stayed with the family; after "Brenda's Got a Baby" came out, we invited Pac to come for our first annual Malcolm X banquet in Atlanta. He showed us the video of "Brenda's Got a Baby." We had him as a youth speaker. Shortly after that, he said he wanted somebody to work with him, that was closer to him. Karen Lee was leaving to work with Prince and had come out of the Black Panther Party out in Jersey. He felt really comfortable with Karen. Since Karen was leaving, he wanted to bring other people in. He brought me in to make up the deficit that was there. Tyehimba Services provided the business management, the personal management, and the public relations for Pac towards the end of '92, beginning of '93. I started managing him toward the end of '92. My company started taking over his affairs about the beginning of 1993.

We had a lot of arguments. What I learned in the process was that you have to let an artist be an artist. You try to give them room to move, creatively, and you try to give them directions. You give them things you want them to look at or read. He read everything. Being influenced by his music was to open my mind to some areas. Some of the things I didn't like what he had to say, and some things

I had to step back and take a closer look at. I hear what you are trying to say, but let's try to do it this way. It was a give-and-take; it wasn't me being influenced by his music. I'm not a young guy that would think Pac was "bad." I'm different. Clearly, he was very creative as an artist. One of the best out there. He was intelligent. He was intelligent stupid. Doing things because he was intelligent but doing stupid things.

We are still talking about him. Young people are still listening to him. When you see people now not saying anything in the music, all you have to do is put a bunch of tattoos on your face and wear gold teeth and halfway dressed like a woman. You're an artist, but Pac had something to say in his music and that was the beauty of it. His music was actually lessons regardless of what he was talking about; he delivers a message in his music, and that was old school. It was the way most artists did it back in the day. People now are reaching back, and realizing some of the lessons that Pac was trying to put out there.

When he stayed with us in LA, the rule was you have to wash the dishes. Everybody must work in this house. He plugged into the family. He was not an artist at that particular time. He was an artist, but he was now a side artist and didn't have all of that. When he became an artist, he recognized that he just had to be a part of the family.

Thug Life was something I didn't support. What Pac was trying to say was he wanted to maintain a relationship with the street owners. That's what he was trying to say. I have had to explain that to so many people. At one point, Mutulu had to actually write a code to Thug Life to try to explain it because he got it permanently on his body. Our pushback was, let's define this for you. Pac gave a bullshit explanation at the Indiana Black Expo, and people ran with it. That was weak because you didn't put any thought into that. We talked about it and I explained that now he has to define it. The Indiana Black Expo was not a deep-thinking explanation of Thug Life. He was trying to say, "Let me deal with the street elements."

His music is still relevant; it's similar to Malcolm. If you listen to Malcolm speak, it's still relevant. That's the long-lasting thing. It's almost like the things he was talking about could be today.

He was a visionary and he didn't think he was going to be here long. Mutulu would often say he was chasing a ghost. When I tried to get life insurance for him, he would say, why? In that sense, he knew his time here was short. And that was really the sentiment of the average young black man in the street, though. He had me listen to this morbid song he was doing. The only fear of death is reincarnation. A lot of things were about death.

Great artist, a very gifted young man. The world lost somebody that today would have been a whole different person. I saw him changing, his growing, I saw all of that. Unfortunately, at twenty-five you haven't got your feet wet. Imagine a fifty-year-old Pac; I see a much calmer, much more centered person. Still that "Pac" energy; I can see a fifty-year-old Pac and not a twenty-five-year-old. Today he would have a greater influence on not only the music but young people in general. He would have been that guiding light for them.

WATANI TYEHIMBA
PI & SECURITY CONSULTANT

WHITNEY-GAYLE BENTA

"Tupac was a real renaissance man. A renaissance man in the sense that he wasn't one-dimensional.
You got a chance to really experience him from different sides."

I WAS FIRST INTRODUCED TO THE MUSIC OF TUPAC THROUGH HIS old group Digital Underground. I remember being a kid and watching *Video Music Box*. I would come home from school and watch tape-recorded videos. I loved Digital Underground with all of the theatrics and color they brought to the visuals and videos. I remember seeing glimpses of Tupac making cameos. At the time I didn't know who he was, to be honest with you. I just knew that he was part of the crew. One thing that really stuck out to me about Tupac was he always looked like he was having a really great time. I asked, "Who is this guy? He's always smiling, having a great time." He did this "In the Same Song" video, which was for a movie soundtrack. That's when I found out he was an MC, too. Whereas I thought he was a hype man and/or a guy part of the crew. That was the moment that solidified him as an artist as well.

Initially, I was mesmerized that they seemed like they were having a good time from "The Humpty Dance" to whatnot. For Digital Underground, what really stuck out for me in terms of being influenced by Tupac was one example, "Brenda's Got a Baby." I distinctly remember it being 1991, I was twelve at the time, a preteen. It was a way of awakening that Brenda could be me. He's telling our stories and he's telling the stories of people from our community. This showed the duality of Tupac being able to have fun on records but also to be the messenger of what's happening in the community. He used his platform to amplify and awaken other people to the struggles that the black community faces.

It's interesting at that time because teen pregnancy was a huge thing. At that particular time, I wasn't sexually active. I had friends and peers that were. I hate to say it, but there was a little bit of shame in terms of society. I was young and confused and really having empathy and being fearful that if somebody I knew in school was having a baby, I don't want them to put their baby in a dumpster. That was a real thing. I didn't know it at the time as I was really, really young. That sent a huge message to me along with Tupac telling people stories.

Tupac created an awakening and really forced people to pay attention to what was going on in the black neighborhoods. As I mentioned, I looked at him as the messenger. We have the message and then he's the messenger. This is what is happening, y'all need to know. We can rap about cars and stuff like that, but he also put action behind it. Not just his words, and that's the difference. Tupac is really doing that, and you see how he was able to affect today because he is often referenced. Even today with it being twenty-five years since he's been gone, people are always referencing him and his work. That is a testament to who he is and his music and how it truly affected people.

The long-lasting effects of his contributions to the world are his art, and not necessarily art in terms of music but that he was an actor. The way he carried himself was art. He was very thought-provoking, and when it came to being photographed for magazines and things of that nature, he was an artist. That's a testament to his background with him going to performing arts school. Tupac was a real renaissance man. A renaissance man in the sense that he wasn't one-dimensional. You got a chance to really experience him from different sides.

I never met him. I will say my favorite memory was a piece of art he created. The magazine where he is lying in the tub with the chains. I thought that was so iconic. I don't know the particulars of how they came to the idea for the creative, but when you think of Tupac, that was one of the images that comes to mind. He was so confident, also, with the jewelry; it was representative of where

I come from. A representation of where we come from as a people. While it may not mean anything to you, it is very symbolic for black people. It means that you've arrived. His face was confident; it was like he was peering at your soul in that photo.

Thug Life is representative of the disenfranchised, the impoverished in black communities. Many cases are ignored in society and they are modern-day warriors. They are fighting in society and in their community to just be seen, appreciated, and valued. At the time, Thug Life wasn't a term people used very often. It was not something that was celebrated. It demonstrated a different meaning, it wasn't so much negative, it was more so from a place of empowerment.

The best way to say it is, black people, keep your head on swivel. We have to stick together, now. With the Black Lives Matter movement, if he were here, he would be at the forefront. He was definitely ahead of his time and definitely wise beyond his years. He had his immature moments like anybody who was in their early twenties.

He was twenty-five when he passed, and you think about people of that age now, they are not necessarily as conscious. I would be remiss if I didn't mention *Judas and the Black Messiah* and that Fred Hampton was twenty-one years old. These kids today want to TikTok. There are definitely a lot of woke young people. But few of the young people today embody the vision that Tupac had at such a young age. He left a blueprint through his music for people to follow. It's a testament to him and his work that people are still talking about him in 2021.

The "California Love" video just popped in my head. One thing that I really loved (and I didn't know Tupac personally, and I don't know if this was something he was promoting because he was on camera), he did seem to really have a great sense of self-confidence, a great sense of self. He was a Gemini, so who knows how many sides he had. He had the Kanye confidence before Kanye, and they are both Geminis.

WHITNEY-GAYLE BENTA
*GLOBAL HEAD OF ARTIST AND
TALENT RELATIONS AT SPOTIFY*

YZ

"When I listen to Pac, it is spiritual or biblical. I don't know why; he just hits differently."

THE FIRST TIME I HEARD OF PAC WAS THROUGH DIGITAL Underground. I was doing a music festival in the Bay area and I remember a bunch of groups, including Digital Underground. When I met Shock G, he introduced me to Tupac, who, when I looked at him, couldn't be stopped; he just kept moving around. Then, fast-forward, they were doing a show, and when Tupac saw me, he approached me and told me to stand by the stage and watch when Digital Underground started "The Humpty Dance," and I didn't know he was going to do this, but he set me up. At one point, they would bring someone on stage to do the dance. So he came and gave me a wedgie. This place is packed, so I chased him around for a couple of seconds and got the joke because everyone was getting a wedgie on the stage.

When Pac moved to Atlanta, I would periodically see him. We could hang out and Pac was always just cool. I remember being on the set of *Above the Rim* with PeeWee, and Pac noticed me and he gave me a huge hug, and at this time I didn't know he and Treach were cool. And I didn't know that the movie scene I saw was what it was and it fucked me up after; I ain't even gonna lie. One other time after that, I saw Pac at an event and he hugged me, but there was no smile. But he seemed to have a lot on his mind. I wanted to talk to him, but by the time I looked up, he was gone. That same day, actually, and this is crazy, I was walking down the street and saw Eazy-E; it was one of the last times I saw him, and *Above the Rim* was the last time I saw Pac, and to lose him was devastating because he was a true gem. So far ahead of his time. Just like Nipsey; he reminded me of Pac. I used to talk to him and think, "You remind me of Pac." Pac was influenced by the freedom-fighter movement. When I looked at Pac, he would get frustrated by things, especially the media, but every time I was around him, he was calm. Every morning I wake up and as I walk to my store, I listen to music... The first song I listen to in the morning is "So Many Tears" every morning, and then "Temptations," then "Dear Mama." And on my walk I pass a mural of Nipsey and say, "Good morning, Nip," and Pac's voice is influential. That dude, his music was honest. You can't say everyone listens to a lot of people and their music is good, but when I listen to Pac, it is spiritual or biblical. I don't know why; he just hits differently. Personally, when Suge helped free Pac or whatever he did, you could tell Pac didn't want to be there. He stayed in the studio and recorded his tracks almost to say all right, I'm good, let me go, I did what I had to do. I think I know what Thug Life meant to Pac. If you come from a certain element of us on the streets. It's a part of us; he was galvanizing us. You got to accept that part of you. People try to give credit to Soulja Boy for being the first on the Internet to blow up; I don't believe that, to me, Pac became the first Internet sensation. I think he knew that, and that's why he was talking crazy when on camera, 'cause you know he wasn't like that. Look at what's happening today; everything is media-based and everything is shocking, and Pac used to be all over the media hard, and it wasn't before the Internet, it was there, it just wasn't like it is now.

YZ
ARTIST & ENTREPRENEUR

AFTERWORD: SEKYIWA KAI SHAKUR

"There isn't one memory of my brother that I can say is the fondest. I miss all of him. I miss the smell of his skin and the sound of his laugh. I miss the banter that we had. I miss the warmth of his touch. There isn't just one fondest memory when you are loved by someone like that. It is a collection of gifted moments."

I SPENT A LOT OF YEARS THINKING ABOUT THE QUESTION, "WHAT do I want people to know about Tupac Shakur?" Especially when he passed. I think about the work I did in the beginning years of the foundation, working on collecting information to share with the world to help people understand his point of view better. As his sister, I felt that he was completely misunderstood. As much as people say that they love him, I still do not believe that he was honored or loved or appreciated enough. That could just be a little sister's point of view, but it is how I feel. I spent a lot of years researching how to help people understand him.

People do not understand who we are. They don't understand how we were raised. They don't understand that we were raised by Uncle Geronimo, who wrote an entire dictionary that we had to learn. We had to learn many new words, and when Tupac would say one thing, the negative connotation that people took it as wasn't what he meant. Today, as a forty-something-year-old, I feel that part of the whole thing was that he was a supernova. He came and he left so early to where you didn't have time to completely understand who he was. You didn't have time to understand what he was about or what he meant. At this age and with my understanding, I no longer act as if I know everything he was or what he meant, but I do know how he inspired me.

My brother took care of all of the children who were younger than him. He was raised to believe that it was his job. It was his job to be a savior for our nation. The Black nation. Him taking care of anybody younger than him, was his charge. Even though we didn't have much. We had less than others growing up. I call it object poverty because we had no objects. There were times when it was just us, crying in the middle of the night with the rats scratching the walls. I would be scared and he would try and comfort me, and in his savior essence, he would promise me that no little kid would have to live like that again. Even in his young age, even being a young man, he tried to wrap his arms around as many children as possible. He was guarded and knew how to give safety and support. He knew how to raise us and develop us and to act as strong, independent, and clear-minded for young and for the old. The generation that raised my generation, they raised us with a lot of fear. That fear paralyzed a lot of us. So, with the seeds that my brother and my mother and my father and my ancestors implanted in me, I take my inner seed, my inner strength, and implant more seeds of empowerment, love, connection, and compassion into another human being. I currently have two biological children, two gifted children, fourteen godchildren, 300 Pac's kids, who are the students of our performing arts center. These are students who have been coming since the moment he passed. Parents bringing their children to us, wanting us to impart anything that was a part of Tupac or part of how he was raised. They wanted us to instill those values into their children.

The times when my family and I reflect and we look at the youth that we call Tupac's kids and we are so moved and so proud of what they are doing in the world. Some of them passed and some of them lived lives just as hard as we did. However, even in the short time that they lived, they left a legacy of hope, love, compassion, and integrity. My biological children were nine and twenty-four months old when he passed. Yet, they beam with pride as well as the struggles and the pain of being a descendent of his. The things that they are doing in the world, the way they love and the way that they emote their pride and their love for their people and their family and their community is just breathtaking to me and makes me feel less lonely. It makes me feel less distant from my brothers.

There isn't one memory of my brother that I can say is the fondest. I miss all of him. I miss the smell of his skin and the sound of his laugh. I miss the banter that we had. I miss the warmth of his touch. There isn't just one fondest memory when you are loved by someone like that. It is a collection of gifted moments. He wasn't the sweetest brother, but he was one of the most loving brothers. He was very hard on me, but he was also very protective in some ways, and yet in other ways, I believe that he allowed the world to have too much access to me. However, as I said, him being a young man, he did the absolute best he could. I wish I could have any of the memories back. Even our fights, running throughout our mother's house, throwing things at each other or him screaming at me to get off the block and go home because it was past my curfew. Even if it was the worst memories that I could have back, I would trade everything for it today. One soft memory of my brother is when he became successful and moved to LA, he made sure that he shared that success with me. Our mother was a classic American lady. She carried herself with elegance and class. That was what my brother wanted for me. He would always make sure I had pearls and diamond studs. He bought me this tennis bracelet when he went shopping with Madonna because he always felt that every woman should have one. He made sure I ate the best, could afford the best, and always had the best.

My understanding now is much different than it was then. Then I wanted to do anything to make sure that people weren't misunderstanding him. Today, I am almost twice my brother's age when he passed. It's completely weird to now be older than your big brother and have information that he didn't have and understand the world differently. The messaging he taught me through his music and communication on how to value myself as a woman, I know better today. I wouldn't listen to him much back then, for example, when he would say something silly like it was okay for your boyfriend to cheat on you, because at least you knew he was real. There was a lot of that messaging that he gave to this world. I love him for that and I see it in so many of my peers. I see a lot of my cousins, who are strong and powerful, and they have so much influence and integrity and they are completing the same story of how Tupac started. I don't see the insecure little boys and girls that I knew growing up in the darkness. They are strong, willing, and prepared, and when I see them, I feel that they are able to be who they are because their cousin, Tupac, did it the way he did and created a space for our people, the way that he did. I am extremely proud of him for it.

Initially when Thug Life came around, me being younger, I understood the sentiment and the point. No matter what we do, in some way we have to be humble and reach back enough to be able to connect to the people who are still on the streets and in our community. We have to be able to answer for the people who are not standing properly. That's what Black Lives Matter should mean, We *matter*. We should act like we matter. We went through four years of trauma. We watched a black man get murdered on television. There were bystanders, people in those buildings, in those windows with guns, but I didn't see a "thug" anywhere. No thug is protecting us. None of that. No gangster is in sight. Their women are being killed in their houses while they sleep and they have no idea what that means. That is a sin to me when so many of my family members fought for the opposite. For Tupac to die in gang violence, in the middle of the street, is a sin to me. It is the opposite of what our family taught me to do and believe in.

Today we have the Black Lives Matter movement, but my brother's death went unsolved. My mother died completely alone and with no support. Even right now, my father is still in prison, past his release date. I am not particularly seeing how my Black family matters. I don't see how we are loving ourselves. THUG Life to me is one of those splinters in my heel. I don't want to post anything or say anything in regards to, because we are so lost in translation, I don't know how to reach the THUG Life people right now. I don't know the words that we are supposed to be using. I don't understand the mindset and how they are thinking they are doing anything masculine. Anything in the name of Tupac, as they are destroying our lives and communities and we do not have anything to depend on. We need to create an infrastructure and reeducate ourselves. We have to learn how to communicate with ourselves. Learn a new language. Learn how to yell and scream at our family members who are leaving with that gun out the house.

I don't want to carry the legacy of Tupac, to be honest. I believe that the foundation of the Shakur family should carry the legacy. My family has been martyrs for our people for decades. I am not into continuing that part of the legacy. Knowing that alone, the weight of life...the weight of the quality of life. The weight of the value of life, we are not a small family. The Shakurs are a breed, an entity. The lessons taught to my brothers and sisters were not just taught to us but to our offspring. So, I don't feel that it is just up to us to carry the legacy of Marcus Garvey or Malcom X or our ancestors. It would be very helpful that our community carry that legacy. It was so comforting to see, in the last few years, so many of us stand up in pride, and that is the legacy of the Shakur family. It shouldn't just be on me and my family alone. The people who are here, who have survived...that is the legacy of my family. Survival. Love. A DUTY to our people.

One of my brother's gifts is that he taught people. He gave people access. He wanted people to believe and understand that he is not the most special. We are all brought here as a gift. He wanted all of us to see our particular gift and beauty and shine with it. He could see a person; to us or everyone else, they may be the weirdest person, but he would see them and want them to know that he sees a light in them. He didn't like signing autographs. When asked for autographs by a person, he would ask them for their autograph. Especially young people. He believed in children and wanted them to know how special they were. He couldn't stand to see a child with sad eyes or a sad heart. The thought of that sadness was his driving force.

"I miss my brother. I miss my family." —Sekyiwa Shakur

SEKYIWA KAI SHAKUR "SET"
SISTER OF TUPAC
PRESIDENT OF THE TUPAC AMARU
SHAKUR FOUNDATION
ENTREPRENEUR

PLAYLIST

1. How Long Will They Mourn Me?
2. Trapped
3. Only God Can Judge Me
4. I Ain't Mad At Cha
5. Changes
6. White Man'z World
7. Soulja's Story
8. Me Against The World
9. Ambitionz Az A Ridah
10. Got My Mind Made Up
11. Bury Me a G
12. I Wonder If Heaven Got a Ghetto (Hip Hop Version)
13. If My Homie Calls
14. Until The End Of Time
15. Pain
16. Do For Love
17. So Many Tears
18. Holler If Ya Hear Me
19. Keep Ya Head Up
20. Pour Out a Little Liquor
21. I Get Around
22. Temptations
23. Picture Me Rollin'
24. Life Goes On
25. Hail Mary

ABOUT THE AUTHOR

Mother, Daughter, Sister, Marketing Executive and Serial Entrepreneur, Aiyisha T. Obafemi is a 31-year veteran for high-profile clients across the music and entertainment sectors. Her zeal for music began at a young age when she traveled the world with her mother who sang with Miriam Makeba and Nina Simone.

In 2001, Aiyisha joined Disturbing Tha Peace Records – a record label owned by renowned entertainer Ludacris and his business partners, Chaka Zulu and Jeff Dixon. Her roles have ranged from Video Commissioner to Marketing Director and Chief Operating Officer.

In her role as Chief Operating Officer and Marketing Director, Aiyisha provided a structured platform for creative idea sharing, establishing a direct link between executives and staff, driving improvements to the brand's product and service offerings and producing integral marketing campaigns.

Aiyisha is currently the CEO/Founder of The Blue Nile Group, Co-Founder of The A&D Agency and Founding Partner of Keeping Score Media, all based in Atlanta, Georgia. Aiyisha is also a board member for The Tupac Amaru Shakur Foundation (TASF).

Coming from a family of revolutionaries, vocalists, and musicians, Aiyisha has taken those elements and applied them to every aspect of her life. Aiyisha will always represent a lineage of strong and intelligent women. Her greatest accomplishment to-date has been raising twin daughters who are blossoming into powerful intellects.

In a male dominated industry, Aiyisha has demanded and earned respect through her unyielding work ethic. She counts on the relationships she has built with her colleagues and tribe of friends for a tight support group. She nurtures her own strengths while constantly helping others build upon their own. She has built a reputation based on perseverance and diligence.

Facebook	@Aiyisha T. Obafemi
Instagram	@AiyishaTheBlessed
Email	Aiyisha67@gmail.com
Twitter	@TheBlessedQueen

The highly anticipated anthology from music industry executive Aiyisha T. Obafemi chronicles and commemorates the societal, and cultural contributions of legendary icon, Tupac Amaru Shakur.

Tupac Amaru Shakur, is unquestionably hailed as one of the most influential rappers of all time. Known to many by his stage names 2pac and Makaveli, his contributions to the entertainment industry and the world as a songwriter and actor consciously shaped the destiny of scores of generations through his unapologetic activism and efforts to shed light against a backdrop of an America in search of justice for all.

Born June 16, 1971, in New York City as the son of Black Panthers, Tupac's destiny was to challenge societal norms that far too often justified inequality and systemic oppression.

Through an offering of poignant, unabridged, stories and anecdotes, *A Light On A Hill* is an unyielding compilation told through the eyes of a vast array of cultural icons and influencers who recognized the heroism in documenting divine wisdom and insight imparted by Tupac prior to his untimely passing.

Candid interviews from Angie Martinez, Bun B, DJ Trauma, Marshawn Lynch, Free Marie, Omari Hardwick, YZ, D-Nice, April Walker, David Banner, Big K.R.I.T., Chaka Zulu, Terri J. Vaughn, Shanti Das, Stephen Hill, Mack Wilds, and more with a moving foreword by Sway Calloway, and afterword by Tupac's sister, Set Shakur serve to further preserve his genius and commemorate his 50th birthday.

13th & Joan is the fastest growing minority owned publishing house, which is dedicated to its mission of cultivating authors and stories that nourish both mind and soul, while leveraging innovative opportunities to engage new generations of readers. The company was formed on October 13, 2015, by Ardre Orie, a Celebrity Ghostwriter who has committed to over three decades as a writing professional. 13th & Joan's clientele includes VH1, MTV, WETV, BRAVO, CENTRIC, YouTube, Grammy Award winning artists, and the NFL as well as a bevy of entrepreneurs and everyday heroes.